IN THE HEADLINES

Journalism

THE NEED FOR A FREE PRESS

THE NEW YORK TIMES EDITORIAL STAFF

Published in 2020 by New York Times Educational Publishing
in association with The Rosen Publishing Group, Inc.
29 East 21st Street, New York, NY 10010

First Edition

The New York Times
Alex Ward: Editorial Director, Book Development
Phyllis Collazo: Photo Rights/Permissions Editor
Heidi Giovine: Administrative Manager

Rosen Publishing
Megan Kellerman: Managing Editor
Hanna Washburn: Editor
Greg Tucker: Creative Director
Brian Garvey: Art Director

Cataloging-in-Publication Data
Names: New York Times Company.
Title: Journalism: the need for a free press / edited by the New York Times editorial staff.
Description: New York : The New York Times Educational Publishing, 2020. | Series: In the headlines | Includes glossary and index.
Identifiers: ISBN 9781642823240 (library bound) | ISBN 9781642823233 (pbk.) | ISBN 9781642823257 (ebook)
Subjects: LCSH: Journalism—Authorship—Juvenile literature. | Reporters and reporting—Juvenile literature. | Journalistic ethics—Juvenile literature. | Mass media—Moral and ethical aspects—Juvenile literature.
Classification: LCC PN4775.J687 2020 | DDC 808'.06607—dc23

Manufactured in the United States of America

On the cover: Journalists take images of Catalan government officials, Sept. 14, 2017; Josep Lago/AFP/Getty Images.

Contents

CHAPTER 6

Press Freedoms in the Trump Era

Introduction

FROM ITS FOUNDING in 1851, The New York Times has set the standard for reporting in the United States and around the world. Initially titled the New-York Daily Times, the newspaper has defined and redefined the nature and importance of press freedoms for over a century. The New York Times has not only provided reports on the regular news and debate regarding the freedom of the press, it has offered a platform for citizens to contribute their own perspectives on the issues, sharing concerns and exercising their First Amendment rights.

Free speech is a central component of not only the U.S. Constitution, but also of journalism. Of course, the opportunity for every person to speak their mind can pose a threat to those with confidential or potentially damaging information. American history is punctuated by wars waged between the news media and the government. When these two entities, entangled and aligned in so many ways, are at odds with each other, it can signify a moment of great instability. What happens when the responsibility of journalists to report the news is at odds with the interests of the government? What happens when the president of the United States starts actively working against the media, frequently vocalizing his disdain for the press and working to discredit publications such as The New York Times?

The Times provides an essential service for the American public; its promise to publish "All the New That's Fit to Print" is a famous motto. What remains up for debate, however, includes what qualifies a story as newsworthy, or the most effective method of communicating that information. Journalists are often able to imbue their reporting with humanity, offering themselves as subjective witnesses to information and allowing their stories to hold an emotional power. This human

JEENAH MOON FOR THE NEW YORK TIMES

The New York Times building in Manhattan. In 2018, the company added 120 newsroom employees, bringing the total number of journalists at The Times to 1,600, the largest count in its history.

perspective can be interpreted as journalistic bias when a reporter or entire staff of reporters approaches a story with a particular, prejudiced perspective. Often, this bias can be presented collectively in the reporting, or lack of reporting, on an issue — for example, the absence of stories in The Times about the devastation of the Holocaust, an issue noted by journalist Max Frankel in his 2001 article, "150th Anniversary: 1851-2001; Turning Away From the Holocaust." Other news outlets have faced controversy and accusations of bias as well: Fox News has been criticized for its misleading coverage of climate change, and in 2018, ABC News had to issue an apology and part ways with their chief investigative correspondent, Brian Ross, due to an errant report involving President Trump and the Russia investigation.

The New York Times has long been perceived as a liberal publication. In fact, as Liz Spayd points out in her 2016 article "Why Readers See The Times as Liberal," "A perception that The Times is biased prompts some of the most frequent complaints from readers. Only they arrive so frequently, and have for so long, that the objections no longer land with much heft." The fissure between The New York Times and right-leaning Americans has only deepened with the arrival of the Trump administration, and the president's unrestrained tirade against what he has deemed "fake news." The fracturing of media in a divided country has raised questions about the future of the industry. What does journalism exist for, and who is the audience?

Journalism is ultimately a business. As newspapers move into the 21st century, they must adapt to changes in how the public engages with journalism, and how these publications generate income. Under the Trump presidency, the pace of news has never been faster, and the demand for content has never been higher. The articles collected in this volume span three centuries of American journalism, offering reflections on the roots of reporting and suggesting what the future holds for the industry.

CHAPTER 1

Defining Freedom of the Press in American Journalism

From its founding, the New-York Daily Times provided a standard for freedom of the press in American journalism. Examining these early articles provides context for the changing nature of censorship and free speech from 1851 on. The newspaper not only reported on instances of controversy regarding press freedoms, but also provided a platform for citizens to share their concerns and exercise their First Amendment rights to speak their minds. The articles in this chapter span 80 years, decades punctuated by regular examination and redefinition of the power and responsibility of journalism.

Journalism.

BY THE NEW YORK TIMES | OCT. 11, 1851

"LET A NEWSPAPER enter a family, and there reiterate, day after day, for a twelvemonth, the most heterodox ideas, and I will warrant a gradual corruption of the family opinions." The frequency and importunity of the attack must produce that result. We underrate the importance of the press, when we reckon it the follower and not the framer of popular sentiments. It is both. Its relation to the popular bias is perfectly reciprocal. It creates occasionally monsters of error, to which, sooner or later, it falls a prey. And, at times it is carried away by gusty and ill-regulated explosions of sentiment, for which it is not responsible, but is always unreasonably held to answer. In all vicissitudes, the Press is a positive power; its influence is direct in advancing its own views, and indirect in developing the current idea of the day. And if we confine its objects to the mere reflection of opinion, we may rest assured we rate its calling at too insignificant a mark.

In England and Germany the tone of the newspaper press has been rather more magisterial and didactic than in France and America. The German editor elaborates a homily day after day, and preaches it into his auditors *ex-cathedra*. His chair is the ideal of a tripod. His words are oracular. He states his proposition as carefully as Spinosa might a metaphysical theorem, and reasons it out according to Quintilian's most approved rules of rhetoric. His pedantry runs into an item, and colors a critique of a ballet-dancer. A volume of essays might be selected from the editorial columns of "Deutschland" *Zeitungs*, not entirely unworthy of a place with selections from British Quarterlies. And throughout the volume the characteristic we allude to would be found a constant quantity; the teaching pertinaciously dogmatical and authoritative.

The London Times, the type of English news literature, is less modest than its cis-atlantic namesake, and dictates opinions as despotically as Stultz the cut of your paletot. Unencumbered with any pecuniary or political fears, it valiantly claims an autocracy of the understanding; a more than papal infallibility. No drifting in the tide of popularity is worth mentioning there. The question once reconnoitred with proper care; its tendencies measured by the rule of a stiff and obstinate conservatism, and irrespective of external influences, the press is unalterably committed. What is true of *The Times*, is relatively true of less important sheets. They assume the air and attitude of dictation, and inculcate their own notions unrestrainedly pro-calculation of what a capricious public may think of them. The English press, from *The Times* down to the smallest country weekly, is vastly more independent and self-reliant than the great body of French and American papers.

In our own country the editor makes less pretension — clothes himself in the garments of humility, and repudiating any design to lead opinion, effectually accomplishes more in directing it, than they do anywhere else out of Paris. In the tumult and conflict of ideas, embracing the rights, interests and duties of so many differing commonwealths and individuals, there must be something for the indolent thinker to pin faith upon. And the majority of thinkers are indolent. One man in ten thousand does his own cogitation, proving his existence by the Cartesian rule, and the rest have a belief in "the paper" for a sole confession of faith. The press, the country more than the city — the weekly more than the daily, does create and rule the prevalent sentiment, and it is the folly of affectation, or the dread of responsibility, that refuses to admit the fact. Such *being* the fact, greatly is the need increased of a more elevated editorial character. Make the press answerable for its emanations, as the sources of immense issues for good or ill, and we shall benefit it infinitely more than by depreciating its power. Its propositions would then be more maturely considered; its language more cautiously measured; and its influence more benignly felt. The editorial of an American paper is usually the warm first impression of a fact, set down at first white heat. The editorial of the German and English *redacteur* is generally a sober, elaborate essay, embracing none but mature results of reflection. When we have borrowed a few of these foreign traits, the press may be equal to its mission. They are needed, and are easily had.

Freedom of the Press.

BY THE NEW YORK TIMES | SEPT. 8, 1861

For the Journal of Commerce.

A FREE PRESS is the cause of great good. Even a licentious Press is far better than a Press which is enslaved, because, in the former case both sides may be heard, but in the latter they cannot. A licentious Press *may* be an evil, but a fettered Press *must* be so.

This is unquestionably true as a general principle, and is most thoroughly and firmly interwoven into the political creed of every free people. Freedom of the Press rests on precisely the same basis as freedom of speech, freedom of opinion, freedom of industry — the full and unfettered right of every individual citizen to seek his own happiness and prosperity in any way which does not infringe the rights or the happiness of anybody else. It is secured to us by the Constitution, and by the unanimous and resistless sentiment of the community. Our people would never tolerate any abridgement of any of these essential and fundamental personal rights — rights of speech, of opinion and of action — except in presence of some overwhelming public necessity — and this is precisely the case now presented.

The Government has, to a certain and very considerable extent, curtailed the freedom of the Press, as well as the freedom of individual opinion and action — and no one can fail to see, in spite of the clamorous outcries of the parties upon whom the interdict falls, that the people thoroughly and heartily approve the act. But this does not by any means imply that the people have become indifferent to their personal rights. It only shows that they are willing to waive those rights for a time, in order to save the Constitution and the Government, from which alone they have any security for those rights in all time to come. Such temporary sacrifices, for the sake of permanent advantages, are of everyday occurrence. That man would be thought a fool who should let his house burn up and perish in the ruins, rather than abandon its shelter for an hour. His *right* to its shelter is perfect; but an Engine Company would have little hesitation in hustling him out and depriving him of his rights, until they could extinguish the flames. A man has a right to smoke a cigar — but not in a powder-magazine. Speech is free — but no man can exercise that freedom in persuading soldiers to desert — or in bargaining for murder, theft or any other crime. Every general principle, in political science, has its limitations — every right, its exceptions. The existence of the Government is in peril; it would be madness to permit men, out of regard for personal freedom, to do or say anything which should aid the work of its destruction. Self-preservation is the first law of Governments, as well as of individuals — and so long as the necessity exists, all minor rights and duties must be held subordinate.

There is no danger to freedom or to personal liberty from this. When the exigency which compels their suppression has passed away, the people will demand their restoration. The alacrity with which they surrender them for the moment must not be taken as an indication of indifference to them. It shows, on the contrary, that they value them too highly to risk their *permanent* destruction, by an unwillingness to waive them for a little time. If this Government is overthrown, civil and political liberty must perish with it. The only guarantee we have for these rights is the Constitution; and the surest way to preserve *them* is by maintaining *it*. The temporary surrender of these rights is a small price to pay for their permanent and perpetual enjoyment.

The Freedom of the Press.

BY THE NEW YORK TIMES | OCT. 19, 1873

THERE IS A DISTINCTION between liberty and license now, as there was in the days when Milton wrote; but it is not always remembered. In the trial of the claimant to the Tichborne estates, the line has been drawn in a very decided manner by the Lord Chief Justice. The editor and proprietor of a provincial paper having chosen to comment upon a part of the evidence for the defense in a manner calculated to influence public opinion as to the guilt of the prisoner, he was summoned to appear before the Court for contempt, and there, after a severe reprimand, he was fined £150 for the offense. The power under which that penalty was inflicted was the power given by the common law, and so far from its having been an attack upon popular liberty, it was, in truth, an action in defense of public justice. If the design of criminal proceedings be to secure the conviction of the prisoner, whether guilty or not guilty, his fate may reasonably be left to the prejudice of any people outside who have the means of making their influence felt. Judges, juries, and all the paraphernalia of a trial, become then a mere empty formality. But if the intention of these institutions be to secure justice, it becomes essential to stop the influence of outside opinion, and to leave the guilt or innocence of prisoners to be decided, where alone it should be decided, in the Courts. Liberty is endangered when men take upon themselves to use the power that has fallen into their hands for the purpose of superseding the action of the Courts, or of influencing the minds of jurymen, and thereby depriving a prisoner of the impartial judgment on the evidence which he has the most perfect right, not only to expect, but to demand.

The public have a right to news; but the prisoner whose life or liberty is at stake, and who, be it recollected, is nothing more than a prisoner till conviction is recorded, has rights also. We may respond to the legitimate demand of the public without assailing the legal claims of the defendant, and hence there is no apology or excuse possible for setting up an extra-legal tribunal in order to prejudge a citizen. Yet the history of the proceedings against every great criminal in this City for a long time past bears evidence of the drag that has been placed upon the wheels of justice by the action of newspaper writers under the impulse of improper motives. For, whether the desire be merely to supply sensational reading to the criminal classes who patronize them, or whether it be to gratify the longings of a malicious prejudice and to influence public sentiment against a prisoner, the offense is the same. One of the first incidents that occurred in the history of the *Polaris*, after the return of a part of the crew, was a persistent effort, by the lengthened publication of illegal evidence, to fix the crime of murder upon one of the party. And the same journal which did that, afterward tried to fasten its offense upon the Executive at Washington, as soon as it discovered that its own object could not be compassed. In the announcement of the Walworth murder, again, the same journal dressed up the fact with two or three columns of a statement pretending to relate every incident that took place in the room while the deed was being done. Every word of that statement was false, and the writer knew that it was false. But the design to prejudge the murderer was the intention, and with certain people "the means justify the end," as young Walworth himself seemed to believe. Once more, and still we refer to the same newspaper, the history of the case of Foster was full of the exercise of the like licentious influence, even to the last. It may not be generally known that a "Commissioner" was sent to Gov. Dix at Albany, a few hours before Foster's execution, to use the influence of his a "paper" against a commutation of the sentence.

While the conductors of newspapers have the indecency and injustice to descend to such proceedings, the interference of the courts becomes necessary; and it is the only means, not of infringing, but of protecting, public liberty. When the day comes upon which the criminal tribunals of the country are inefficient exponents of the law, it may be necessary to devise some other means for the protection of society and the punishment of criminals; but the improper exercise of newspaper authority such as we have referred to, is an insult to the courts and an injustice to the accused, which it would be well if our Judges were to stop with a strong hand, similar to that shown under our own common law by the Chief Justice of England.

A Candid Opinion.

FROM THE NEW-YORK SUN | NOV. 1, 1875

THE OUTSPOKEN THREAT of Mr. John Kelly to prosecute The New-York Times for libel, after the election, is a political act of no little significance. It gives us a clear view of the standard of principles by which Tammany Hall is to be gauged in the event of its coming into full power as the result of this election. Mr. Kelly expects to have the courts and the District Attorney's office under his thumb.

We have no attack to make upon Mr. Kelly, except so far as he exhibits himself by his public acts and in the present campaign. Recorder Hackett was thrown over by Tammany on the ground that, in certain criminal cases, he made judicial decisions in favor of a certain individual, obnoxious to Tammany Hall as now organized, though formerly its leader. What is the plain and irresistible logical inference from this? Is it not the clearest and most emphatic notice to all the Judges on the bench that if they wish to have the support of Tammany Hall, and if they wish to retain their offices, they must decide all questions, even of personal rights and criminal law, as Tammany Hall wishes and dictates? And was ever before such a dangerous, such an atrocious doctrine propounded in this free country?

If Mr. Kelly succeeds in fully establishing his power by the election of next Tuesday, it is assuming a good deal to conclude that the freedom of the press will be maintained here by any easy or ordinary struggle. It is not impossible for Grand Juries and Petit Juries to be so manipulated by District Attorneys as to direct indictments and verdicts in certain channels. We should look to see civil suits for libel supplemented by criminal prosecutions, and with a Judge on the bench swift to do the bidding of Tammany Hall, it would be a thing not at all surprising to us to see the guardians of the public rights consigned to the jail and the Penitentiary. The most faithful friends of liberty have met such fates before, and why may they not he subjected to them again?

There can be no possible occasion for a libel suit or a prosecution against The New-York Times. If in the most heated political discussion that journal says anything of any man untrue and unjust, he has only to lay clear evidence of this before the proprietors to have it retracted and the matter set right. We assume to say this because we know the proprietors of that paper to be gentlemen, and we know that the high character of that journal could not be maintained by any other rule and practice. We say, therefore, that so far as The New-York Times is concerned, no aggrieved individual ever has any real occasion to resort to the law of libel. He can get redress, if he is entitled to it, easier and quicker.

We were not surprised yesterday morning to learn that practical effect had been given to Mr. Kelly's intentions to silence the press by an attempt to get the editors of The Times arrested on the complaint of one King — appropriate name for the first effort to assert despotic power!

Mr. Ecclesine appears in this proceeding as attorney. It may he our duty to our neighbors of The Times to inform them that Mr. Ecclesine is by no means without experience in the same line. He once brought a suit against the *Sun* for the publication of an infamous letter of William H. Kemble, which Mr. Kemble swore he never wrote; but unfortunately Mr. Kemble had sworn on a previous occasion that he did write the same letter! There was a little disparity between his two oaths which he could not explain.

Mr. Ecclesine on that occasion had arranged to go to a dinner party in the evening, where he was to receive the congratulations of his friends on his victory; but the honest jury refused to give him a verdict even for six and a quarter cents, and he concluded to stay away from that dinner!

We apprehend that Mr. Ecclesine's proceedings before the Magistrate in his new case will hardly bear close criticism. We doubt whether there is any legal evidence — and no other is admissible in such a proceeding — that Messrs. Jennings and Jones are the publishers of The

Times. Mr. Ecclesine, we think, has been a little too fast; but we only refer to this point as showing the recklessness of the attorney.

Then, again, it seems that Mr. Ecclesine openly proclaimed that he had a political, partisan object to accomplish in instituting this prosecution. Is such the business of a reputable lawyer? Is not this perverting the law to base uses, to which it should never be brought?

The attack on The Times is an assault on the freedom of the press. In that fight, from Alpha to Omega, we are with The Times, out and out, and against John Kelly, and all the other enemies of liberty, from the beginning to the end.

The Freedom of the Press.

BY THE NEW YORK TIMES | MAY 30, 1917

WHAT IS COMMONLY called the freedom of the press is not inherently its special right or privilege. The phrase is only another name for the freedom of speech, which is the right of the people to communicate one with another. Freedom of the press, therefore, derives its standing from the fact that the press is pre-eminently the medium for this interchange. Since the press, commanding the service of every other means of communication, is the common carrier of information, delivering it almost instantly and simultaneously throughout a nation, and there is no other carrier a thousandth part so efficient, any restriction upon the information it may convey deprives every citizen in some degree of capacity for intelligent thought and wise action. This is obviously of greatest importance in relation to the affairs of government and that is why, since its vital connection with the welfare of peoples has been understood, the freedom of the press has been so jealously guarded no more by its own servants than by the statesman, the publicist, and the enlightened citizen. Political writers have generally agreed during the last century that liberty of the people cannot long survive without freedom of the press. Only the autocrat, aware that popular ignorance is the strongest entrenchment of his power, and the bureaucrat, who would screen incompetency and corruption, have dissented.

Although the freedom of speech and the freedom of the press are the same, in order that no technicality may be invoked to differentiate them and thus deprive speech of its chief means of utterance, both are specifically mentioned in the Constitution as beyond the power of Congress to abridge. The wording of the First Amendment is: "Congress shall make no law respecting an establishment of religion, or prohibiting the free exercise thereof, or abridging the freedom of speech, or of the press." In what does this freedom consist, and what would constitute its abridgment? Certainly the freedom prescribed in the amendment is not freedom to commit crime. The test of the freedom of the press is public welfare. It may publish what the public is entitled to know. It may not violate copyright, it may not comment on court proceedings in a way to prejudice a cause at bar, it may not libel; above all, it may not, in time of war, willfully communicate to an enemy information that would facilitate the enemy's hostile operations.

The last of these offenses is treason, already punishable by law, and it is the only one that need be considered here. In every one of the twenty-nine futile attempts by Congress to formulate a press censorship law the basis has been the law of treason, accompanied by an indefinite qualification. This qualification, in whatever form it appears, invariably hands over to another authority the power to extend at will the definition of treason and to supervise or forbid publication. This is the abridgment of the freedom of the press that is expressly inhibited by the Constitution. In effect, it sets up a power of intimidation. The purpose of the proposed law is not punishment, for that is provided in existing law, but interference and coercion before any crime is committed or contemplated.

Censorship therefore places in the hands of appointive officers, almost invariably of little or no experience in public affairs or in relation to the press, an almost limitless power of oppression. How this power would be used in this country is foreshadowed by the rules and regulations made public by the so-called Committee on Public Information. The rules are perhaps harmless enough — most of them have been voluntarily observed by the newspapers during the last two months; it is the interpretation of them that reveals what may be expected should this committee be endowed with the authority which it does not now possess. We are informed, for example, that the Department of State disapproves of "discussion of differences of opinion between the Allies and difficulties with neutral countries," "speculation about possible peace," and anything "likely to prove offensive to any of the Allies or to neutrals." Under this regulation, what would become of the news from Russia, Holland, Denmark and Scandinavia, now freely published, even in the countries accustomed to censorship? And no discussion of possible peace! How soon after a censorship law was passed would this advice and wide extensions of it be translated into commands, supported by every agency of coercion that could be brought to bear? No danger then of the revelation to the people of the shortcomings of men in office!

Apart from its unconstitutionality, censorship may be set down as a futility in the present situation of the United States. Our journals cannot reach the enemy until from two to six weeks after publication, and they might be withheld altogether from the outgoing mails rather than deprive our own people of legitimate information. It may be supposed that their contents could be cabled or communicated by wireless telegraph, but a check is put upon this by the Government's control of these means of communication, supplemented by similar control in France and Great Britain. Beyond all this, our enemies cannot, except by the indiscretion of Government officials, procure information that is not accessible to anybody who seeks it. When the American destroyers sailed for England the newspapers and a considerable part of the public knew it, but the newspapers kept their knowledge to themselves. This did not prevent communication of the news to Germany by agents not yet hampered by the Government's belated control of the cables. In this instance the Government should have been able to keep the knowledge within its own circle.

The Secretary of the Navy has also complained of the currency of various disturbing rumors. This is one of the first consequences of the mere threat of press censorship. The newspapers are receiving letters reciting these rumors and accusing them of suppressing the truth. An actual censorship would breed further rumors; anonymous circulars and pamphlets professing to give the real truth, but designed to serve enemy purposes, would spring up, with consequences upon the public mind impossible to estimate.

The press has its shortcomings, it is often in error, but it is loyal and patriotic, and it is the voice of the people. Whatever confusion of counsel it may seem at times to offer, somewhere the right word is always spoken, gains attention and authority, and becomes the fixed policy of the people, to which the statesman must bow. We do not believe Congress will attempt to stifle the speech of the people.

Free But Responsible.

BY THE NEW YORK TIMES | JUNE 3, 1931

FOR SOME WEEKS past the Supreme Court of the United States has been a source of stirring news. Not dry judicial decisions on abstract points of law but opinions dealing with vital questions of individual rights and liberties have been successively coming from that court. The latest is not least in importance. Speaking for the majority of the Supreme Court, Chief Justice Hughes has laid down principles, now the law, respecting the freedom of the press in this country which are at once a safeguard and a warning for American newspapers. The decision is, in effect, that they are free to publish what they honestly think, but that they cannot avoid responsibility, whether social or legal, for what they print.

The case grew out of the much-discussed Minnesota statute. That State law provided for the abatement, as a public nuisance, of any "malicious, scandalous and defamatory newspaper, magazine or other periodical." Enacted in 1925, it was brought into force against a Minneapolis paper, The Saturday Press. Chief Justice Hughes summarized the procedure by stating that it enabled the judge, without a real trial, to suppress a newspaper and to make its further publication "punishable as a contempt." Appeal was taken to the Minnesota courts, where the statute was sustained as constitutional. That decision is now reversed by the Supreme Court of the United States on the ground that the law in question was really one to establish a censorship of the press, and was in violation of the rights guaranteed by the Constitution of the United States.

That the Minnesota statute, now held invalid, struck at a real evil Chief Justice Hughes did not deny. In his summation of the facts and the arguments before the court he spoke in tones which were scathing, but not too much so, in condemnation of reckless, unscrupulous and defamatory journalism. He fully admitted the existence of "miscreant purveyors of scandal " in the press, but insisted that the lawful remedies against them lie elsewhere than in a "previous" censorship. That is to say, after publication the responsible persons can be duly tried and punished. If they flaunt obscenity, the police can come down upon them. If they preach sedition or advocate overthrow of this Government, the appropriate statutes can be snapped upon them like handcuffs. If they viciously assail the character of individuals, whether in public office or in private life, they can be made to answer by the laws of libel.

Undoubtedly there are mischievous abuses of the freedom of the press. Judge Hughes feels them keenly and specifically denounces them. But he is convinced that the larger and lasting benefits of liberty of opinion and of publication outweigh all the grievances that can be alleged in such cases as were held to justify the Minnesota law, and that nothing must be done to impair the protection of the press against censorship and restraint upon publication. However reprehensible the conduct of any newspaper may be, "the theory of the Constitution guarantee is that even a more serious public evil would be caused by authority to prevent publication."

For the public as well as for the press, it was of the highest importance that this case should have been carried to the Supreme Court of the United States. Its decision will amply reward those who saw from the first the peril which lay in this Minnesota law, and spent time and money in bringing about a test of it before the Supreme Court. Chief among these was Colonel McCormick of Chicago, who has placed the entire newspaper profession in his debt. But no editor or publisher should infer that this weighty and conclusive judicial decision yields the slightest warrant for unlimited license in printing scandalous or defamatory matter. The freedom of the press, now again happily vindicated and affirmed, is not freedom to be a "chartered libertine." With the liberty freely to think and utter goes a constant and grave responsibility. It is a responsibility partly to public opinion, partly to the law. It should be, above all, a responsibility to a newspaper's own conscience. That cannot be violated without incurring automatically penalties graver than any which a hastily devised statute could inflict.

CHAPTER 2

Defying Censorship and the Legacy of the Pentagon Papers

On June 30, 1971, the Supreme Court overturned the Nixon administration's effort to prevent The New York Times and The Washington Post from publishing the Pentagon Papers, a top-secret account of the Vietnam War. What distinguished this defense of the First Amendment from others was that the ruling allowed The Times to provide not just interpretive articles, but the actual classified documents themselves. In arguing for the rights of the press, this landmark ruling drew upon the 1931 case of Near v. Minnesota, in which the Supreme Court ruled against a Minnesota law that curtailed journalistic freedoms. The articles in this chapter detail the process and outcome of both these cases, and reflect upon the lasting importance of these rulings.

The Covert War

BY THE NEW YORK TIMES | JUNE 13, 1971

THE PENTAGON PAPERS disclose that in this phase the United States had been mounting clandestine military attacks against North Vietnam and planning to obtain a Congressional resolution that the Administration regarded as the equivalent of a declaration of war. The papers make it clear that these far-reaching measures were not improvised in the heat of the Tonkin crisis.

When the Tonkin incident occurred, the Johnson Administration did not reveal these clandestine attacks, and pushed the previously prepared resolution through both houses of Congress on Aug. 7.

Within 72 hours, the Administration, drawing on a prepared plan, then secretly sent a Canadian emissary to Hanoi. He warned Premier Pham Van Dong that the resolution meant North Vietnam must halt the Communist-led insurgencies in South Vietnam and Laos or "suffer the consequences."

The section of the Pentagon study dealing with the internal debate, planning and action in the Johnson Administration from the beginning of 1964 to the August clashes between North Vietnamese PT boats and American destroyers — portrayed as a critical period when the groundwork was laid for the wider war that followed — also reveals that the covert military operations had become so extensive by August, 1964, that Thai pilots flying American T-28 fighter planes apparently bombed and strafed North Vietnamese villages near the Laotian border on Aug. 1 and 2.

Moreover, it reports that the Administration was able to order retaliatory air strikes on less than six hours' notice during the Tonkin incident because planning had progressed so far that a list of targets was available for immediate choice. The target list had been drawn up in May, the study reports, along with a draft of the Congressional resolution — all as part of a proposed "scenario" that was to build toward openly acknowledged air attacks on North Vietnam.

Simultaneously, the papers reveal, Secretary McNamara and the Joint Chiefs of Staff also arranged for the deployment of air strike forces to Southeast Asia for the opening phases of the bombing campaign. Within hours of the retaliatory air strikes on Aug. 4 and three days before the passage of the Congressional resolution, the squadrons began their planned moves.

'PROGRESSIVELY ESCALATING PRESSURE'

What the Pentagon papers call "an elaborate program of covert military operations against the state of North Vietnam" began on Feb. 1, 1964, under the code name Operation Plan 34A. President Johnson ordered the program, on the recommendation of Secretary McNamara, in the hope, held very faint by the intelligence community, that "progressively escalating pressure" from the clandestine attacks might eventually force Hanoi to order the Vietcong guerrillas in Vietnam and the Pathet Lao in Laos to halt their insurrections.

In a memorandum to the President on Dec. 21, 1963, after a two-day trip to Vietnam, Mr. McNamara remarked that the plans, drawn up by the Central Intelligence Agency station and the military command in Saigon, were "an excellent job."

"They present a wide variety of sabotage and psychological operations against North Vietnam from which I believe we should aim to select those that provide maximum pressure with minimum risk," Mr. McNamara wrote.

President Johnson, in this period, showed a preference for steps that would remain "noncommitting" to combat, the study found. But weakness in South Vietnam and Communist advances kept driving the planning process. This, in turn, caused the Saigon Government and American officials in Saigon to demand ever more action.

Through 1964, the 34A operations ranged from flights over North Vietnam by U-2 spy planes and kidnappings of North Vietnamese citizens for intelligence information, to parachuting sabotage and psychological-warfare teams into the North, commando raids from the sea to blow up rail and highway bridges and the bombardment of North Vietnamese coastal installations by PT boats.

These "destructive undertakings," as they were described in a report to the President on Jan. 2, 1964, from Maj. Gen. Victor H. Krulak of the Marine Corps, were designed "to result in substantial destruction, economic loss and harassment." The tempo and magnitude of the strikes were designed to rise in three phases through 1964 to "targets identified with North Vietnam's economic and industrial well-being."

The clandestine operations were directed for the President by Mr. McNamara through a section of the Joint Chiefs organization called the Office of the Special Assistant for Counterinsurgency and Special Activities. The study says that Mr. McNamara was kept regularly informed of planned and conducted raids by memorandums from General Krulak, who first held the position of special assistant, and then from Maj. Gen. Rollen H. Anthis of the Air Force, who succeeded him in February, 1964. The Joint Chiefs themselves periodically evaluated the operations for Mr. McNamara.

Secretary of State Dean Rusk was also informed, if in less detail.

The attacks were given "interagency clearance" in Washington, the study says, by coordinating them with the State Department and the Central Intelligence Agency, including advance monthly schedules of the raids from General Anthis.

The Pentagon account and the documents show that William P. Bundy, the Assistant Secretary of State for Far Eastern Affairs, and John T. McNaughton, head of the Pentagon's politico-military operations as the Assistant Secretary of Defense for International Security Affairs, were the senior civilian officials who supervised the distribution of the schedules and the other aspects of interagency coordination for Mr. McNamara and Mr. Rusk.

The analyst notes that the 34A program differed in a significant respect from the relatively low-level and unsuccessful intelligence and sabotage operations that the C.I.A. had earlier been carrying out in North Vietnam.

AIR RAIDS WERE PLANNED JOINTLY

The 34A attacks were a military effort under the control in Saigon of Gen. Paul D. Harkins, chief of the United States Military Assistance Command there. He ran them through a special branch of his command called the Studies and Observations Group. It drew up the advance monthly schedules for approval in Washington. Planning was done jointly with the South Vietnamese and it was they or "hired personnel," apparently Asian mercenaries, who performed the raids, but General Harkins was in charge.

The second major segment of the Administration's covert war against North Vietnam consisted of air operations in Laos. A force of propeller-driven T-28 fighter-bombers, varying from about 25 to 40 aircraft, had been organized there. The planes bore Laotian Air Force markings, but only some belonged to that air force. The rest were manned by pilots of Air America (a pseudo-private airline run by the C.I.A.) and by Thai pilots under the control of Ambassador Leonard Unger.

Reconnaissance flights by regular United States Air Force and Navy jets, code-named Yankee Team, gathered photographic intelligence for bombing raids by the T-28's against North Vietnamese and Pathet Lao troops in Laos.

The Johnson Administration gradually stepped up these air operations in Laos through the spring and summer of 1964 in what became a kind of preview of the bombing of the North. The escalation occurred both because of ground advances by the North Vietnamese and the Pathet Lao and because of the Administration's desire to bring more military pressure against North Vietnam.

As the intensity of the T-28 strikes rose, they crept closer to the North Vietnamese border. The United States Yankee Team jets moved from high-altitude reconnaissance at the beginning of the year to low-altitude reconnaissance in May. In June, armed escort jets were added to the reconnaissance missions. The escort jets began to bomb and strafe North Vietnamese and Pathet Lao troops and installations whenever the reconnaissance planes were fired upon.

The destroyer patrols in the Gulf of Tonkin, code-named De Soto patrols, were the third element in the covert military pressures against North Vietnam. While the purpose of the patrols was mainly psychological, as a show of force, the destroyers collected the kind of intelligence on North Vietnamese warning radars and coastal defenses that would be useful to 34A raiding parties or, in the event of a bombing campaign, to pilots. The first patrol was conducted by the destroyer

Craig without incident in February and March, in the early days of the 34A operations.

SEPARATE CHAIN OF COMMAND

The analyst states that before the August Tonkin incident there was no attempt to involve the destroyers with the 34A attacks or to use the ships as bait for North Vietnamese retaliation. The patrols were run through a separate naval chain of command.

Although the highest levels of the Administration sent the destroyers into the gulf while the 34A raids were taking place, the Pentagon study, as part of its argument that a deliberate provocation was not intended, in effect says that the Administration did not believe that the North Vietnamese would dare to attack the ships.

But the study makes it clear that the physical presence of the destroyers provided the elements for the Tonkin clash. And immediately after the reprisal air strikes, the Joint Chiefs of Staff and Assistant Secretary of Defense McNaughton put forward a "provocation strategy" proposing to repeat the clash as a pretext for bombing the North.

Of the three elements of the covert war, the analyst cites the 34A raids as the most important. The "unequivocal" American responsibility for them "carried with it an implicit symbolic and psychological intensification of the U.S. commitment," he writes. "A fire-break had been crossed."

The fact that the intelligence community and even the Joint Chiefs gave the program little chance of compelling Hanoi to stop the Vietcong and the Pathet Lao, he asserts, meant that "a demand for more was stimulated and an expectation of more was aroused."

WARNING BY THE JOINT CHIEFS

On Jan. 22, 1964, a week before the 34A raids started, the Joint Chiefs warned Mr. McNamara in a memorandum signed by the Chairman, Gen. Maxwell D. Taylor, that while "we are wholly in favor of executing the covert actions against North Vietnam ... it would be idle to conclude that these efforts will have a decisive effect" on Hanoi's will to support the Vietcong.

The Joint Chiefs said the Administration "must make ready to conduct increasingly bolder actions," including "aerial bombing of key North Vietnam targets, using United States resources under Vietnamese cover," sending American ground troops to South Vietnam and employing "United States forces as necessary in direct actions against North Vietnam."

And after a White House strategy meeting on Feb. 20, President Johnson ordered that "contingency planning for pressures against North Vietnam should be speeded up."

"Particular attention should be given to shaping such pressures so as to produce the maximum credible deterrent effect on Hanoi," the order said.

The impelling force behind the Administration's desire to step up the action during this period was its recognition of the steady deterioration in the positions of the pro-American governments in Laos and South Vietnam, and the corresponding weakening of the United States hold on both countries. North Vietnamese and Pathet Lao advances in Laos were seen as having a direct impact on the morale of the anti-Communist forces in South Vietnam, the primary American concern.

This deterioration was also concealed from Congress and the public as much as possible to provide the Administration with maximum flexibility to determine its moves as it chose from behind the scenes.

The United States found itself particularly unable to cope with the Vietcong insurgency, first through the Saigon military regime of Gen. Duong Van Minh and later through that of Gen. Nguyen Khanh, who seized power in a coup d'état on Jan. 30, 1964. Accordingly, attention focused more and more on North Vietnam as "the root of the problem," in the words of the Joint Chiefs.

Walt W. Rostow, the dominant intellectual of the Administration, had given currency to this idea and provided the theoretical framework for escalation. His concept, first enunciated in a speech at Fort

Bragg, N.C., in 1961, was that a revolution could be dried up by cutting off external sources of support and supply.

Where North Vietnam was concerned, Mr. Rostow had evolved another theory — that a credible threat to bomb the industry Hanoi had so painstakingly constructed out of the ruins of the French Indochina War would be enough to frighten the country's leaders into ordering the Vietcong to halt their activities in the South.

'NO LONGER A GUERRILLA FIGHTER'

In a memorandum on Feb. 13, 1964, Mr. Rostow told Secretary of State Rusk that President Ho Chi Minh "has an industrial complex to protect: he is no longer a guerrilla fighter with nothing to lose."

The Administration was firmly convinced from interceptions of radio traffic between North Vietnam and the guerrillas in the South that Hanoi controlled and directed the Vietcong. Intelligence analyses of the time stated, however, that "the primary sources of Communist strength in South Vietnam are indigenous," arising out of the revolutionary social aims of the Communists and their identification with the nationalist cause during the independence struggle against France in the nineteen-fifties.

The study shows that President Johnson and most of his key advisers would not accept this intelligence analysis that bombing the North would have no lasting effect on the situation in the South, although there was division — even among those who favored a bombing campaign if necessary — over the extent to which Vietcong fortunes were dependent on the infiltration of men and arms from North Vietnam.

William Bundy and Mr. Rusk mentioned on several occasions the need to obtain more evidence of this infiltration to build a case publicly for stronger actions against North Vietnam.

The accompanying article, as well as the rest of the series on the Pentagon's study of the Vietnam war, was a result of investigative reporting by **NEIL SHEEHAN** of The New York Times Washington bureau. The series has been written by Mr. Sheehan, **HEDRICK SMITH**, **E. W. KENWORTHY** and **FOX BUTTERFIELD**. The articles and documents were edited by **GERALD GOLD**, **ALLAN M. SIEGAL** and **SAMUEL ABT**.

The Freedom to Speak

OPINION | BY SAM J. ERVIN JR. | OCT. 3, 1971

WASHINGTON — One of the historical lessons that the American people seem always to have difficulty learning is the truth of the warning enunciated so long ago: "Eternal vigilance is the price of liberty." We can never rest on the laurels won by our ancestors, nor can we delude ourselves into thinking that our liberties, once having been obtained, are forever secure.

The Founding Fathers had experience with the tyranny over freedom that results from prior restraints. Out of that experience came the First Amendment which, without question, has been understood for almost two hundred years to prohibit government-inspired injunctions against publishing by the press. Yet in the excitement and crisis of the Pentagon Papers episode, this understanding was once again questioned by the Justice Department.

Events now transpiring in Boston before a Federal grand jury put into question another principle of freedom. I have in mind, of course, the efforts of the Administration to inquire into the actions of the junior Senator from Alaska, Mr. Gravel, in connection with the revelations of the contents of the Pentagon Papers. [He] convened a subcommittee, of which he is chairman, and proceeded to read into the committee record the contents of the Pentagon Papers. The action of the Senator from Alaska was a demonstration of personal courage. Whether it was foolish, unauthorized, or should be condoned by the Senate is another question. But this is a question for the resolution of the Senate, not by another body.

It is apparent, however, that the Administration now seeks to impose its own judgment on the Senator, and to punish him for his actions. A grand jury is conducting a broad inquiry into how these papers were obtained and released to the press. The Government also seeks, it appears, to inquire into the actions of the Senator from

Alaska and the speech he made before his subcommittee. It undoubtedly wants to know how he got his copies of the Pentagon Papers. In pursuit of this aim, it has subpoenaed the Senator's aide, Dr. Leonard Rodberg, to testify, and even asserted the right to subpoena the Senator himself.

Of course, the Administration is really arguing that it may tell a Senator when and where and in what manner, and with what information, he may discuss the war in Vietnam. The Administration would say that Senators must only comment on issues germane to a committee meeting, as it would determine "germane." If the germaneness rule applies, that means that the Government or a private person can peruse committee transcripts, seeking to find remarks not within the scope of the subject of the hearing. Congressmen and Senators will have to watch what they say lest it be claimed that it is not germane, and so opens them up to harassment, law suits and prosecutions.

The tendency, if not the intent, of this effort is to silence critics in this body along with those who are outside these halls. This action is of a pattern we have seen recently. The private citizen must fear Army spies and the Subversive Activities Control Board which will retaliate against Administration critics; the press must fear injunctions and treason charges should it publish facts which are secret only because they are embarrassing; and now Senators must face subpoenas of themselves and their aides. Even officials within the Administration are threatened with the insult of the lie detector if unkind or critical information leaks out.

The Administration is not slow to assert its own privileges, even when they do not exist, and even when the claim interferes with the responsibilities of this body under the Constitution.

They will not produce Army generals to testify about Army surveillance.

They will not produce Dr. Kissinger to testify about foreign policy.

They will not produce State Department plans which explain our foreign aid policy.

They will not tell us what the standards are for putting a citizen into an internal security computer.

The affairs of the executive branch are hidden from the scrutiny of the Congress and the American people. But if a Senator should dare to offend those in power by disclosing to the American people information improperly kept secret by the executive branch, then it claims the right to haul him before the grand jury and make him testify. The logical next step would be to assert a right to prosecute the Senator for making the speech, on the ground that it contained stolen information.

The past actions of the Administration raise considerable doubt regarding its appreciation of the constitutional rights of Americans. They suggest that the Administration does not understand that there are limits to its powers.

There is growing evidence that the Administration cannot tolerate criticism. Many citizens already fear it will act against its critics to prevent them from speaking if it can and to punish them thereafter if necessary.

The action taken against the Senator from Alaska, by the subpoena of his aide and the threats against the Senator himself, adds to these fears and suspicions, just as the attempt to secure injunctions against the press added to them earlier in the summer.

This article is excerpted from remarks by Senator **SAM J. ERVIN JR.** of North Carolina, chairman of the Subcommittee on Constitutional Rights.

A 45-Year-Old Rivet in the First Amendment

OPINION | BY FRED W. FRIENDLY | JUNE 9, 1976

ALTHOUGH JOURNALISTS TEND to give all credit to the Founding Fathers for freedom of the press, it was the creative work of this century's judiciary — Charles Evans Hughes, Oliver Wendell Holmes, Louis D. Brandeis, Harlan F. Stone and Owen J. Roberts — that reinforced the prohibition against prior restraint and, in effect, nationalized the First Amendment when they decided Near v. Minnesota 45 years ago this month.

In 1925, the Minnesota State Legislature passed a public nuisance bill that permitted the state to close down a newspaper or magazine that was "obscene, lewd, lascivious ... or maliciously scandalous and defamatory." Two years later, a small Minneapolis scandal sheet, the Saturday Press, was silenced by a restraining order sought by the Hennepin County prosecutor, Floyd B. Olsen. The publishers, Jay M. Near and Howard Guilford, self-admitted scandalmongers and occasional blackmailers, had charged that Jewish gangsters were controlling gambling and bootlegging in Minneapolis: "Practically every vendor of vile hooch ... every snake-faced gangster and embryonic yegg in the Twin Cities is a JEW. ... It is Jew, Jew, Jew, as long as one cares to comb over the records." Olsen was among the politicians accused of being a pawn of the Jewish conspiracy.

The county judge forbade the Saturday Press "to produce, edit, publish, ... sell or give away any publication." His order was upheld five months later when the Minnesota Supreme Court declared that "sincere and honest" publications were protected by the law, but that "our Constitution was never intended to protect malice, scandal and defamation." The case might have ended there had not Col. Robert R. McCormick of The Chicago Tribune committed $35,000 and his own law firm to fight the case.

When Near v. Minnesota was argued in the United Slates Supreme Court, Justice Brandeis, himself a Jew, asked the most probing questions. "It is difficult to see," observed Mr. Brandeis, "how one is to have a free press ... without the privilege this Minnesota Act seems to limit. These editors seek to expose coordination between criminals and public officials profiting from gambling ... you are dealing here with scandal that ought to be a matter of prime interest to every citizen."

"Assuming it to be true," argued James E. Markham for the state of Minnesota.

"No," Justice Brandeis snapped back. "A newspaper cannot always wait until it gets the judgment of a court. These men set out on a campaign to rid the city of certain evils."

"So they say," Mr. Markham interrupted.

"Yes, of course, so they say," answered Justice Brandeis. "They acted with courage. They invited suit for criminal libel if what they said was not true." The justice concluded, "Now if that campaign was not privileged, if that is not one of things for which the press exists, then for what does it exist?"

Those present when Near was argued sensed it would be a close call. Justice Pierce Butler of Minnesota read lengthy anti-Semitic quotations from the Saturday Press and argued that the gag order was not a prior restraint. He saw nothing in the Constitution to prevent the banning of lewd or malicious defamation. Justice Holmes sided with Justice Brandeis.

Chief Justice Hughes, the swing vote in the 1931 decision that overturned the Minnesota law, wrote the opinion: "The fact that for one hundred and fifty years there has been almost an entire absence of attempts to impose previous restraints upon publication ... is significant of the deep-seated convictions that such restraints would violate constitutional rights." To require a publisher to prove in a court of law truth without malice before publication "is the essence of censorship."

The Court, however, was careful to state that the First Amendment is not absolute. Among the few limitations on the free press were publication of such secrets as sailing dates of troop ships during war and of obscenity.

In the 45 years since Near, the Court has held the line against further extensions of prior restraints on the reporting of news and opinion. In the 1971 Pentagon Papers case, the Supreme Court refused to grant an injunction sought by the Nixon Administration, but the Court is now deliberating the constitutionality of a gag order that could alter that precedent. Some morning this month the nine Justices are expected to tell us whether the alleged abuses of pre-trial news coverage of a Nebraska murder case compel a redefinition of the right of free press or whether Chief Justice Hughes's rejection of prior restraints still stands.

FRED W. FRIENDLY, Edward R. Murrow Professor of Journalism at Columbia University, is author of "The Good Guys, the Bad Guys and the First Amendment."

At Home Abroad; Freedom of the Press

OPINION | BY ANTHONY LEWIS | JUNE 7, 1981

FIFTY YEARS AGO this month the Supreme Court decided the great case, Near v. Minnesota, that breathed life into the First Amendment's guarantee of press freedom in this country. Ten years ago, daring to test that freedom on the sensitive issue of the Vietnam War, The New York Times began printing the Pentagon Papers — and won in the Supreme Court when the Government tried to stop publication.

The anniversaries of those legal landmarks are worth celebration, and reflection. For time has brought clarifying light to bear on both episodes. We can see now, I think, that they were not so much victories for the press as for a political experiment, the one begun in 1776.

At the heart of the American system is the idea that the people are sovereign: not in some theoretical sense, but actually having the power and the duty to control their government. Other countries have freedom, but none subjects its government to such intimate and continuing public accountability. The American public, to play its constitutional role, must be informed. And that is what the legal tests of June 1931 and June 1971 were about.

The Near case is known for establishing the American legal presumption against "prior restraints." Under the First Amendment, the Supreme Court held, courts cannot ordinarily stop publication of something because it may be false or damaging — not even the nasty Minnesota weekly involved in the case, the Saturday Press, which specialized in abuse of politicians and anti-Semitic diatribes.

But there was more to the case, and more to the Saturday Press, than that. So we find in a fascinating new book on the case, "Minnesota Rag," by Fred W. Friendly.

For all its abusiveness, the Saturday Press did actually dare to print stories about gangsters and their links to politicians that more respectable papers did not. And a lot of the stories were true. Only the Saturday Press, for example, wrote about a gangster attack on Sam Shapiro's dry-cleaning store because Sam would not pay for "protection." The story forced a prosecution, and Sam's 11-year-old son Irving was a principal witness. He went on to become chairman of the Du Pont Company.

The Supreme Court, when it considered the case, well understood the significance of the press's role in informing the public about what Chief Justice Hughes's opinion called "official malfeasance and corruption." At the argument Justice Brandeis said the editors of the Saturday Press had acted with "great courage" in challenging "criminal combinations." He asked:

"How else can a community secure protection from that sort of thing if people are not allowed to engage in free discussion?" When 40 years later The New York Times started to publish the Pentagon Papers, it was asking essentially the same question. Only this time free discussion was needed to expose not local crime or corruption but years of deception by national leaders that had got the United States mired in a terrible war.

Just as the State of Minnesota had claimed that it needed to protect its citizens from the "scandalous" writings of Jay M. Near and his weekly, so the United States Government said it had to protect the country from the disclosures of the Pentagon Papers. Officials witnesses predicted the most appalling damage to the national security if the history collected in the Papers were allowed out.

William B. Macomber, Deputy Under Secretary of State, testified — in a court hearing held in secret because of the alleged sensitivity of the evidence — that diplomatic disclosures in the Papers might "undermine our relations" with allies. If the U.S. could not have confidential communications with other governments, he said, "we have irreparably damaged the chance of free government to endure."

Floyd Abrams, a lawyer who helped represent The Times in 1971, took a retrospective look at the Pentagon Papers case in a piece for today's New York Time's Magazine. Among others he interviewed Mr. Macomber, now President of the Metropolitan Museum. Mr. Macomber said he thought it was right for the Government to bring the case but thought it was "probably decided properly" against suppression. He said:

"Even though I've been a diplomat all my life and nothing is more important to me than the security of the United States, the First Amendment is, in another way, the security of the United States. You can't save something and take the heart out of it."

The official attitudes evident in 1931 and 1971 are just the same today and always will be. Those who are in office think they know best. Nowadays hardly any judge would try to restrain disclosures of local scandal. But Federal officials are inventing new ways, under the guise of "national security," to keep the public from knowing about life-and-death issues of policy.

At the heart of the First Amendment — really of the entire Constitution — is an open relationship between governors and the governed. It is still an experiment: a dangerous one. But it is our system.

ANTHONY LEWIS is an Op-Ed columnist for The New York Times.

Colonel McCormick to the Rescue

REVIEW | BY NEAL JOHNSTON | JULY 12, 1981

MINNESOTA RAG

The Dramatic Story of the Landmark
Supreme Court Case That Gave New Meaning
to Freedom of the Press.
By Fred W. Friendly.
Illustrated. 243 pp. New York: Random House. $12.95.

MOST LAW SUITS contain the ingredients of good stories. When the bar sits down to drink, passion, principle and money are the stuff of the best tales. Hardly any dispute ever actually goes to trial unless there is real fervor pushing at least one side forward, and by the time a case reaches the Supreme Court of the United States there is an immense amount of passion motivating all parties to the argument. But no one reads court opinions to find out what was really going on, for they are all cool principle: The passion leaks out between the footnotes.

In "Minnesota Rag," Fred Friendly, a former television executive, Ford Foundation official and professor of journalism at Columbia, has set out to tell the forgotten story of Near v. Minnesota, a 1931 Supreme Court case that is the critical wellspring of modern First Amendment law. The story is rich and bizarre. The principles were, and are, of first importance. Just 10 years ago, The New York Times won the Pentagon Papers case, resisting the Federal Government's effort to block publication of those portentous documents. The Times probably could not have won without the help of Jay Near, a sleazy and shadowy operator who, in the fall of 1927, published nine issues of an anti-Semitic scandal sheet that also happened to include some articles exposing local corruption and labor racketeering — until he was put out of business by the Minneapolis city fathers.

The Minnesota courts, applying freshly manufactured state law, held that as a fit punishment for the defamation already published in his paper, Near should be forever enjoined from producing any more issues of his rag. This, the judges reasoned, was not prior restraint; this was just justice. There was little in the way of legal precedent to the contrary.

Somehow the unlikely figure of Near attracted the attention and the passionate interest of a most colorful and implausible savior: Colonel Robert R. McCormick, the truculent, xenophobic and all-in-all preposterous publisher of The Chicago Tribune. McCormick managed to see the now obvious fact that the gagging of Near threatened all newspapers, most certainly including his own. McCormick's surprising perspicacity may have been aided by his recent run of litigation with two powerful enemies: Henry Ford and "Big Bill" Thompson, the Republican mayor of Chicago. Ford and Thompson each would have been delighted to sue The Tribune shut. Colonel McCormick was no man's lieutenant, and he seized control, essentially pushing Near out of the case, save for the caption. The matter was carried to Washington, and the Supreme Court eventually held the Minnesota gag law unconstitutional. Near could be punished, perhaps, for what he had written, but he could not be silenced for the future.

Most people seem to think that the First Amendment to the Federal Constitution guarantees to all Americans — even the Jay Nears — the right to say what they want, when they want, with utter impunity. As with most important things, it is not so simple.

The First Amendment itself merely prohibits Congress from abridging freedom of speech and of the press. The Amendment doesn't purport to restrict the states, many of which went abridging merrily along. It was not until 1925 that the Supreme Court even hinted that the First Amendment might restrict the states as a result of the 14th Amendment requirement that the states respect the due-process rights of all Americans. Indeed, there basically was no First Amendment case law until the 1920's. For the first 150 years, neither the

Court nor the American people seemed to care very much what the Amendment meant.

Unthinkable as it may be today, back when Near was first raking his muck, it was a seriously debated issue whether the First Amendment provided any protection at all from a state statute such as the one used to suppress Near. Near v. Minnesota helped settle that question.

The Court has never held offensive behavior to be legally immune simply because the central act was the speaking or printing of words. Libel is the standard example of a kind of speech that may be punished, but blackmail, attempted extortion, conspiracy to fix prices and perjury are other examples of essentially verbal acts that are criminal beyond the concept of freedom of speech and press.

Furthermore, "freedom of speech" is not a self-defining concept. Rather, it is what lawyers love to call a "term of art" — a handle for a complex bundle of essentially artificial concepts. The First Amendment does not promise that all speech will be free but only forbids government to abridge the sorts of speech that fit within the technical construct "freedom of speech."

Fifty years ago it was an open question whether the freedom-of-speech concept encompassed the act of publishing defamation and scandal. The five-Justice majority in Near v. Minnesota provided a definitive answer: Since government corruption cannot be exposed without defaming the corrupt, since public scandal cannot be revealed without scandalous revelation, the vital function of the press can only be protected if the right to publish scandal and defamation is itself protected by the Constitution.

This conclusion seems self-evident to us now, but we have lived with its consequences for half a century. The four-man minority saw a different meaning, adopting Justice Joseph Story's flat contention that the Amendment meant no more than that "every man shall be at liberty to publish what is true, with good motives and for justifiable ends." With one more vote, that would have become the law, and by today we might have learned to adjust to a very different set of First Amendment consequences.

Mr. Friendly includes the text of the Supreme Court's opinion in Near v. Minnesota, both Charles Evans Hughes's majestic majority statement and Pierce Butler's somewhat prissy dissent. Butler's opinion is the more important to read today: It is wrong, narrow and very foreign, but it has its internal logic, and it almost represented the winning side. The most important lesson to be drawn from this book is that the decision in Near v. Minnesota was, in every sense, a close call.

Given the quality of the story, it is unfortunate that Mr. Friendly doesn't tell it better. The difficulty arises from excessive ambition. In a very short book, he tries to cover everything, and as a result too little comes alive. He moves us from the ore-dusted brothels of Duluth, Minn., to the gothic top of the Tribune Tower, to the cloistered conference room of the Supreme Court. He tries to explicate everything from the gangster-ridden politics of Prohibition-era Minnesota to the rarified politics of Herbert Hoover's appointments to the Court. Probably it is impossible, in a mere 180 pages, to explain both American legal process and Colonel Robert McCormick to the modern reader.

NEAL JOHNSTON is a practicing attorney who was formerly the secretary of the Association of the Bar of the City of New York.

1971 | Supreme Court Allows Publication of Pentagon Papers

TIMES INSIDER | BY DAVID W. DUNLAP | JUNE 30, 2016

Times Insider shares historic insights from The New York Times. In this piece, David Dunlap, a Metro reporter, reflects on the 45th anniversary of the historic victory for freedom of the press.

"WE AGREE."

Not among the most stirring judicial defenses of the First Amendment you've ever heard. But it was enough to get the job done.

On June 30, 1971, the Supreme Court overturned the Nixon administration's effort to restrain The New York Times and The Washington Post from publishing a top-secret history of the Vietnam War called the Pentagon Papers.

Its unsigned opinion, in which six justices concurred, simply quoted from two other decisions ("Any system of prior restraints of expression comes to this court bearing a heavy presumption against its constitutional validity" ... the government "thus carries a heavy burden of showing justification for the imposition of such a restraint") before reaching this understated conclusion:

> *The District Court for the Southern District of New York, in The New York Times case, and the District Court for the District of Columbia and the Court of Appeals for the District of Columbia Circuit, in The Washington Post case, held that the government had not met that burden. We agree.*

Joyful editors in New York ordered the immediate resumption of publication, which had been on pause since June 15, under court order. The Times had managed to print three installments of the series, which it called the "Vietnam Archive," before the government effectively shut it down, leaving much of the exposé unpublished.

What distinguished the Pentagon Papers was that The Times was not only providing interpretive articles, but also presenting the

BARTON SILVERMAN/THE NEW YORK TIMES

Neil Sheehan at his desk in the newsroom.

documents themselves, which had been leaked by Daniel Ellsberg, a military analyst who had worked on the history. These included cablegrams, memorandums, drafts of policy papers, instructions, transcripts and the like.

"The documents are the written words of the men who set the armies in motion and launched the warplanes," Neil Sheehan, the chief reporter of the series, said. "The written words are immutable, engraved now in the history of the nation for all to examine."

But publishing classified documents about the prosecution of a war, even though they were at least three years old at the time, was bound to rouse the government.

"The Joint Chiefs are likely to believe that, for the integrity of the security of their procedures, they must act," Harding F. Bancroft, the executive vice president of The Times, cautioned Arthur Ochs Sulzberger, the publisher, in a memo on June 10.

Later that day, Mr. Sulzberger — to his everlasting credit, at least in journalists' hearts — told the managing editor, A. M. Rosenthal, to go ahead with the full series, documents and all. He had one little complaint. "I feel that the stories I saw were still overwritten and unnecessarily complicated," Mr. Sulzberger said. "I strongly recommend a very sharp blue pencil."

(The newsroom apparently failed to appease him. Mr. Sulzberger later complained, good-naturedly, "Until I read the Pentagon Papers, I did not know that it was possible to read and sleep at the same time.")

The White House pounced on Monday, June 14, at 8:34 p.m., when a telex arrived at The Times, addressed to Mr. Sulzberger, over the signature of Mr. Nixon's attorney general, John N. Mitchell:

"I have been advised by the secretary of defense that the material published in The New York Times on June 13, 14, 1971, captioned 'Key Texts from Pentagon's Vietnam Study,' contains information relating to the national defense of the United States and bears a top secret classification," he began — without even a hope-this-finds-you-well.

"As such, publication of this information is directly prohibited by the provisions of the Espionage Law, Title 18, United States Code, Section 793.

"Moreover, further publication of information of this character will cause irreparable injury to the defense interests of the United States.

"Accordingly, I respectfully request that you publish no further information of this character and advise me that you have made arrangements for the return of these documents to the Department of Defense."

Instead, The Times advised the Justice Department that it had no plans to comply.

"The Times must respectfully decline the request of the attorney general, believing that it is in the interest of the people of this country to be informed of the material contained in this series of articles," the newspaper said in a statement. "We have also been informed of the attorney general's intention to seek an injunction against further publication. We believe that it is properly a matter for the courts to decide. The Times will oppose any request for an injunction for the same reason that led us to publish the articles in the first place. We will of course abide by the final decision of the court."

The injunction came the next day in a complaint that named as defendants the seven reporters and editors credited with the series and the 15 executives listed on the newspaper's masthead. John Crewdson and Barbara Dubivsky of the Washington bureau quickly came up with a retort, printing hundreds of buttons that said, "Free The Times XXII" and "Free The Times 22."

To the astonishment of everyone involved, the case made its way to the Supreme Court in less than two weeks. Oral arguments by The Times's legal team, headed by Alexander M. Bickel, were heard on Saturday, June 26.

The subsequent 6-to-3 decision was something of a muddle. In their haste to decide a fast-moving case, the justices barely had time to write their own concurring or dissenting opinions, much less build the consensus needed for a unified voice.

Nonetheless, the resolution of the Pentagon Papers case seemed to blunt prior restraint as a government tool for dealing with stories it does not want you or me to read. The most prominent exception was a 1979 case in which the government tried to prevent the Progressive magazine from publishing an article about the hydrogen bomb, said George Freeman, the executive director of the Media Law Resource Center.

That's not to say that the White House hasn't tried to use prior restraint since then.

Much newsroom drama preceded the publication on Dec. 16, 2005, of an article by James Risen and Eric Lichtblau that exposed the Bush administration's use of warrantless wiretaps. At a meeting in the White House, President George W. Bush himself had tried to persuade The Times's publisher, Arthur Sulzberger Jr., and its executive editor, Bill Keller, to kill the story.

He had no more luck doing so than Mr. Mitchell had in 1971.

But a chilling prospect emerged after the White House meeting. "The administration, I was told, had considered seeking a Pentagon Papers-type injunction to block publication of the story," Mr. Lichtblau wrote for Slate, in an adaptation of his book, "Bush's Law: The Remaking of American Justice."

"The tidbit was a bombshell," Mr. Lichtblau wrote. "Few episodes in the history of The Times — or, for that matter, in all of journalism — had left as indelible a mark as the courtroom battle over the Pentagon Papers, and now we were learning that the Bush White House had dusted off a Nixon-era relic to consider coming after us again."

Mr. Risen described to Times Insider what happened next.

"Eric was told about the plans for a court injunction, told me and the editors, and we ran the story that same night. Keller decided to post the story online early, at 7 p.m. that night — virtually unheard of in 2005 — to get the story out before the White House could seek an injunction," Mr. Risen wrote. "It was clear to me that The Times

TYRONE DUKES/THE NEW YORK TIMES

After the Supreme Court handed down its decision on June 30, 1971, the composing room prepared to resume publication of the Pentagon Papers series.

reacted so swiftly to run the story immediately because they saw this as the same situation as the Pentagon Papers."

That may have spelled the end to prior restraint even more effectively than the 1971 court decision.

"The administration might be able to stop the presses with an injunction," Mr. Lichtblau wrote, "but they couldn't stop the internet."

The Pentagon Papers Team Tells How The Times Defied Censorship

TIMES INSIDER | COMPILED BY NANCY WARTIK | JAN. 20, 2018

Times Insider shares historic insights from The New York Times.

FOUR ALUMNI OF The New York Times met Tuesday on Facebook Live to recount the dramatic events surrounding our 1971 publication of the Pentagon Papers, a watershed moment in the history of press freedom.

The Washington Post's publication of the Pentagon Papers returned to the national spotlight with the release last week of the feature film "The Post." But The Times was the first to publish portions of the Papers, starting June 13, 1971. We published three articles over a period of two days before a federal court ordered us to stop. On July 1, 1971, we resumed publication after winning a landmark Supreme Court decision.

During Tuesday's Facebook Live, the Times alumni described the secrecy surrounding their work on the Papers and their frustration with the public's initial reaction to our publication. Here are some excerpts from their conversation, condensed and edited for clarity.

David Dunlap: *I'm David Dunlap, I'm a retired reporter at The New York Times and I have gathered today four very distinguished New York Times alumni who are also alumni of the Pentagon Papers.*

I've brought them together so that we can talk about what's wrong and what's right with the new Steven Spielberg movie "The Post," but more importantly to tell the very dramatic story of how the Pentagon Papers were obtained, developed, produced, edited, curated, published against the threat of tremendous legal liability from the Nixon administration — a dramatic enough story in itself that would have made, we believe, for a very good movie called "The Times."

TERESA ZABALA/THE NEW YORK TIMES

From left to right: Jeff Schmalz, Eileen Butler, Allan Siegal and Lou Jordon in 1975.

I'm going to ask them to introduce themselves in the order in which they first came into contact with the Pentagon Papers in the late spring of 1971. Allan Siegal?

Allan Siegal: I'm Allan Siegal. I was, at the time, an assistant foreign editor. I was called upon to join the team that was gathering to edit the stories and texts.

Linda Amster: My name is Linda Amster, I was the head of news research at The Times and I was brought in very early on in the preparation of the Pentagon Papers to make sure that all of the material we published was accurate. That was my main responsibility.

Betsy Wade: My name is Betsy Wade, I came into the Pentagon Papers project a week before publication began, when Al Siegal asked me if I wanted to join Project X, and did I mind going to jail?

James Goodale: My name is James Goodale. I first came in contact with the Pentagon Papers when I was at this fancy black-tie dinner in Washington, D.C., male only by the way, and [NYT Washington bureau chief] Max Frankel whispered into my ear, "Have you heard, we've got classified documents?" That was it. One sentence. But those documents turned into the Pentagon Papers.

Dunlap: *The importance of the classified documents is critical to this discussion because what The Times had in its possession were 7,000 pages of documents that were a top-secret, classified history of American involvement in Vietnam, in Indochina, going back to the Truman administration, every page of which had been stamped "top secret," "sensitive," "classified."*

Part of the mission of The Times was to present the history of the Vietnam War as it had been recorded under the orders of then-Secretary of Defense Robert McNamara who wanted to find out, how did we get into this mess?

The people who compiled the report had access to all kinds of cables, memos and notes, which betrayed — when you read them closely — that one administration after the next had engaged in exactly the kind of double-dealing that critics of the war had always maintained was going on. But here was the Pentagon saying it, in its own voice.

Because of that, it was critical, as far as The Times saw it, to reproduce the documents themselves. Not simply interpret them or rely on them for narrative articles, but to actually expose the public to the words of the decision makers. And that meant that we were trading in classified information on a scale that perhaps had never been undertaken before.

What kind of pause did that give any of you as you worked with this material?

Amster: Well, I was among the first people to join the team and I knew nothing about it. It was very early on.

When I was taken to the Hilton Hotel where the team was working on the papers — not in the headquarters of The Times but in the hotel — I was told that we had these papers and it was of course against the law to have these papers and it could even be treasonous to have these papers, and if I did not want to work on them, I was free not to work on them.

And of course I wanted to work on them, but right off the bat it was clear that imprisonment was a possibility and I'm sure everybody else felt that way too.

Goodale: Well, the documents caused me problems. I'm a lawyer.

The Pentagon Papers were split into documents, and into regular text. The regular text, in fact, was based on New York Times articles, no problem. I warned everybody at the beginning that it's going to be a lot more dangerous to publish the regular text, if you leave the documents out. And that ignited a huge argument within The Times in which the news people finally said, "If you don't run the documents, you're not going to run anything."

From a personal point of view, when I read the material to be published and I had a chance to read the documents that had been picked out, I remember reading one particularly from national security adviser and strong proponent of the war McGeorge Bundy that shocked me. And I said this has got to be published, the public has never seen anything like this. Go with the documents.

Dunlap: *I have a question from a viewer. ... Yes, thank you for the question. A viewer wants to know: "Has the culture for whistle-blowers changed in the last half-century?"*

Goodale: If we take all of the whistle-blowing we've had in the last decades, I would say that Daniel Ellsberg, the military analyst who originally gave the Papers to The Times, set the gold standard for whistle-blowing. If you say that's the best you can do, I think subsequent whistle-blowing has been more or less at his level. To answer the question: I don't think it's changed. It's been very good.

Dunlap: *I might propose a distinction. And that is to make the point to viewers that The Times, very importantly, spent three months with these 7,000 pages of documents. And among our goals, it seems to me, besides presenting as cohesive a narrative as we could from these documents, was to ensure that military secrets that would compromise the identity of C.I.A. agents, for example, that would put into harm's way any troops, that such material not be published.*

I think perhaps you could draw the distinction between the very careful in essence curation of a classified document against the dumps that we now see with WikiLeaks and other sources that just put the material out there, consequences be damned.

Goodale: Well I think that there is something in what you say. But I think we have to be careful when we paint WikiLeaks with a big, bad brush because the first WikiLeaks leak that became notorious, was one that was curated.

The New York Times got Wikileaks's materials. It curated them. It didn't publish all of them. There were other papers, The Guardian included, that did the same thing. And then after they had done what they had done, WikiLeaks changed what it was going to deliver to the public and curated itself.

I would admit, however, as we look at what's taken place thereafter, WikiLeaks has been more of a "dump" than it was before. But you have to be careful how you describe that.

Dunlap: *Now, in a discussion that all of us had just before the Facebook session, several of us spoke of a marvelous affidavit that was filed in the Pentagon Papers case by Max Frankel, who was then the Washington bureau chief, in which he described in some detail the way in which reporters and government officials routinely traded in classified information. It was absolutely the coin of the realm.*

The only problem that government officials seem to have with classified information is when it doesn't paint them in the light they'd like to be painted in. Otherwise they trade in it with impunity, it seems.

Goodale: Can I comment on Max Frankel's affidavit? Max Frankel wrote an affidavit in which he described how information is traded, even though it's classified. And the ultimate conclusion of that statement is that classification in the real world means zero.

You might be interested in the history of that affidavit. Max had a lawyer assigned to him — we had five lawyers in the case; I was running the case, and we signed different parts of it — and he didn't like the lawyer, who was a perfectly capable, competent lawyer.

And Max would say what you just implied in your statement, to this lawyer. And the lawyer would say, "It can't be! It can't be that people really don't pay attention to the classification stamp!" Argument, back and forth, back and forth. It was very important to turn that lawyer. Because if a lawyer didn't turn around and reflect our point of view, it was going to come through in what he said.

And Max finally threw up his hands. He said, "I'll write an affidavit." So he wrote this affidavit, in which he describes how this works in the real world. All the stuff that's traded back and forth is classified because everything's classified. "When everything's classified" — I'm quoting the Supreme Court — "nothing is classified."

Wade: When I was being indoctrinated on the foreign desk, Al Siegal said, "You know what "classified" means? Classified means you put them in some kind of order, any kind of order, alphabetical, numerical." [Laughter] He said, "top secret, now we're talking about something." And for many years, the foreign desk did not use classified to mean "secret" or "not to be distributed." It had to be further modified. Am I not correct, boss?

Siegal: I don't remember, to be perfectly honest. But I do know that we were careful not to wave the red flag of "classified" around in the paper. Because the feeling was that stories that you could write with perfect impunity would suddenly become controversial within the government if you rubbed their nose in the fact that you were flouting classification.

DONALD F. HOLWAY/THE NEW YORK TIMES

Betsy Wade at her desk in 1969.

Dunlap: *Some other questions have come in.*

Facebook viewer Jauhn Asfar Awraghr: *How did you work with so many documents? Nowadays we have USB keys or laptops but how did you do that, then? Were you driving a minivan with all the files?*

Wade: We were carrying shopping bags through Times Square, between The New York Times and the Hilton Hotel, among other things, trying to appear as innocent as possible. Some of them were grocery carts.

Siegal: And using more people than we would have had to use nowadays.

Dunlap: *And it was also the case that basically an independent and secret newsroom was established in the New York Hilton Hotel, a* *place so anonymous that as Mr. Siegal has observed on more than one occasion:*

Siegal: You could lead a camel through the lobby of that hotel on a tether, and nobody would take note.

Dunlap: *And so it appeared that for all of our weeks there, with dozens and dozens and dozens of staff members, with filing cabinets and typewriters, our presence was not detected.*

Facebook viewer David W. Jones: *When preparing the publication of the Pentagon Papers, was there much discussion on how the public was expected to react?*

Wade: The beginning was a terrible disappointment to us. Nobody leaped up and said, "They stole those things! These are stolen documents!" Silence.

Siegal: And nobody leaped up and said, "The government lied to the public for all of these many years." And I think we went into it expecting that there would be a large public reaction against government deceit. Some of that developed but it developed slowly.

Amster: And while I was working on it, I kept thinking that the publication of the papers would soon lead to the end of the Vietnam War because there was so much damning material about Lyndon Johnson and John F. Kennedy. And I thought Nixon would take advantage of that to try to end the war — I didn't take into account his paranoia and other reasons for suing The Times.

Dunlap: *I want to reflect one last question as we wrap up.*

Facebook viewer Lynn Moffat: *Can the panel discuss technology's role in changes that have affected the national secrecy system and the role of journalists?*

RENATO PEREZ/THE NEW YORK TIMES

Linda Amster, the director of The Times's news research desk, in 1971.

Dunlap: *And I would also append to that question, the notion that the internet now perhaps makes possible the publication of information with less of an eye on being enjoined by the government.*

When The Times has seen that threat approaching, as it did with the Risen and Lichtblau story, the notion is, get it up on the web before they even try to stop us. So I'll put that to you. Technology: How has that changed the reporting of classified information?

Amster: Well it's certainly changed the research involved in doing something like the Pentagon Papers. This is pre-Google, pre-any electronic source of information available and so it really relied on printed matter, mostly. Which was the clipping file, the huge New York Times morgue and also books, magazines, that kind of thing. I think it would be much easier now and quicker to get the information it took so long to get, to verify that.

Siegal: But also much harder, if you want to consider something as crass as a newspaper's competitive position, much harder to keep secrets and keep an exclusive, exclusive.

Amster: Within the newsroom itself, everyone was quite aware that something was going on, but nobody knew what. I think there's no question about it that with social media that would have leaked out so quickly. It would have been very evident that The Times was working on something and it might have curtailed our ability to prepare the Papers.

Dunlap: *So while it's true the Pentagon Papers might have fit easily into a thumb drive, we wouldn't have been able to keep that a secret for very long at all. I thank Allan Siegal, Linda Amster, Betsy Wade and James Goodale for talking about The New York Times's role in the Pentagon Papers.*

CHAPTER 3

Addressing Bias and Controversy

When a story is covered unevenly, or not covered at all, how can a newspaper reconcile that? From a discussion of the disturbing lack of Holocaust coverage, to an examination of the perception of The Times as a left-leaning publication, the articles collected in this chapter demonstrate the biases, or perceived biases, that have been acknowledged in the coverage of a variety of stories. The articles in this chapter illustrate the way bias presents itself, the subsequent controversy that can arise and the effort on the part of The Times and other media outlets to address these instances of supposed partisan reporting.

The Times and Wen Ho Lee

BY THE NEW YORK TIMES | SEPT. 26, 2000

ON MARCH 6, 1999, The New York Times reported that Government investigators believed China had accelerated its nuclear weapons program with the aid of stolen American secrets. The article said the Federal Bureau of Investigation had focused its suspicions on a Chinese-American scientist at the Los Alamos National Laboratory. Two days later, the government announced that it had fired a Los Alamos scientist for "serious security violations." Officials identified the man as Wen Ho Lee.

Dr. Lee was indicted nine months later on charges that he had transferred huge amounts of restricted information to an easily accessible computer. Justice Department prosecutors persuaded a judge to hold him in solitary confinement without bail, saying his release would pose a grave threat to the nuclear balance.

This month the Justice Department settled for a guilty plea to a single count of mishandling secret information. The judge accused prosecutors of having misled him on the national security threat and having provided inaccurate testimony. Dr. Lee was released on the condition that he cooperate with the authorities to explain why he downloaded the weapons data and what he did with it.

The Times's coverage of this case, especially the articles published in the first few months, attracted criticism from competing journalists and media critics and from defenders of Dr. Lee, who contended that our reporting had stimulated a political frenzy amounting to a witch hunt. After Dr. Lee's release, the White House, too, blamed the pressure of coverage in the media, and specifically The Times, for having propelled an overzealous prosecution by the administration's own Justice Department.

As a rule, we prefer to let our reporting speak for itself. In this extraordinary case, the outcome of the prosecution and the accusations leveled at this newspaper may have left many readers with questions about our coverage. That confusion — and the stakes involved, a man's liberty and reputation — convince us that a public accounting is warranted.

In the days since the prosecution ended, the paper has looked back at the coverage. On the whole, we remain proud of work that brought into the open a major national security problem of which officials had been aware for months, even years. Our review found careful reporting that included extensive cross-checking and vetting of multiple sources, despite enormous obstacles of official secrecy and government efforts to identify The Times's sources. We found articles that accurately portrayed a debate behind the scenes on the extent and importance of Chinese espionage — a debate that now, a year and a half later, is still going on. We found clear, precise explanations of complex science.

MIKE FIALA/AFP/GETTY IMAGES

Former Los Alamos nuclear scientist Wen Ho Lee addresses the media outside the Federal Courthouse after he was freed from nine months of solitary confinement, Sept. 13, 2000, in Albuquerque, N.M.

But looking back, we also found some things we wish we had done differently in the course of the coverage to give Dr. Lee the full benefit of the doubt. In those months, we could have pushed harder to uncover weaknesses in the F.B.I. case against Dr. Lee. Our coverage would have been strengthened had we moved faster to assess the scientific, technical and investigative assumptions that led the F.B.I. and the Department of Energy to connect Dr. Lee to what is still widely acknowledged to have been a major security breach.

The Times neither imagined the security breach nor initiated the case against Wen Ho Lee. By the time our March 6 article appeared, F.B.I. agents had been looking closely into Dr. Lee's activities for more than three years. A bipartisan congressional committee had already conducted closed hearings and written a secret report unanimously concluding that Chinese nuclear espionage had harmed American national security, and questioning the administration's vigilance. The

White House had been briefed repeatedly on these issues, and the secretary of energy had begun prodding the F.B.I. Dr. Lee had already taken a lie detector test; F.B.I. investigators believed that it showed deception when he was asked whether he had leaked secrets.

The Times's stories — echoed and often oversimplified by politicians and other news organizations — touched off a fierce public debate. At a time when the Clinton administration was defending a policy of increased engagement with China, any suggestion that the White House had not moved swiftly against a major Chinese espionage operation was politically explosive.

But the investigative and political forces were converging on Dr. Lee long before The Times began looking into this story.

The assertion in our March 6 article that the Chinese made a surprising leap in the miniaturization of nuclear weapons remains unchallenged. That concern had previously been reported in The Wall Street Journal, but without the details provided by The Times in a painstaking narrative that showed how various agencies and the White House itself had responded to the reported security breach.

The prevailing view within the government is still that China made its gains with access to valuable information about American nuclear weaponry, although the extent to which this espionage helped China is disputed. And while the circle of suspicion has widened greatly, Los Alamos has not been ruled out as the source of the leak.

The article, however, had flaws that are more apparent now that the weaknesses of the F.B.I. case against Dr. Lee have surfaced. It did not pay enough attention to the possibility that there had been a major intelligence loss in which the Los Alamos scientist was a minor player, or completely uninvolved.

The Times should have moved more quickly to open a second line of reporting, particularly among scientists inside and outside the government. The paper did this in the early summer, and published a comprehensive article on Sept. 7, 1999. The article laid out even more extensively the evidence that Chinese espionage had secured the key design elements of an American warhead called the W-88 while showing at the same time that this secret material was available not only at Los Alamos but "to hundreds and perhaps thousands of individuals scattered throughout the nation's arms complex."

That article, which helped put the charges against Dr. Lee in a new perspective, appeared a full three months before the scientist was indicted.

Early on, our reporting turned up cautions that might have led us to that perspective sooner. For example, the March 6 article noted, deep in the text, that the Justice Department prosecutors did not think they had enough evidence against the Los Alamos scientist to justify a wiretap on his telephone. At the time, the Justice Department refused to discuss its decision, but the fact that the evidence available to the F.B.I. could not overcome the relatively permissive standards for a wiretap in a case of such potential gravity should have been more prominent in the article and in our thinking.

Passages of some articles also posed a problem of tone. In place of a tone of journalistic detachment from our sources, we occasionally used language that adopted the sense of alarm that was contained in official reports and was being voiced to us by investigators, members of Congress and administration officials with knowledge of the case.

This happened even in an otherwise far-seeing article on June 14, 1999, that laid out — a half year before the indictment — the reasons the Justice Department might never be able to prove that Dr. Lee had spied for China. The article said Dr. Lee "may be responsible for the most damaging espionage of the post-cold war era." Though it accurately attributed this characterization to "officials and lawmakers, primarily Republicans," such remarks should have been, at a minimum, balanced with the more skeptical views of those who had doubts about the charges against Dr. Lee.

Nevertheless, far from stimulating a witch hunt, The Times had clearly shown before Dr. Lee was even charged that the case against him was circumstantial and therefore weak, and that there were numerous other potential sources for the design of the warhead.

There are articles we should have assigned but did not. We never prepared a full-scale profile of Dr. Lee, which might have humanized him and provided some balance.

Some other stories we wish we had assigned in those early months include a more thorough look at the political context of the Chinese weapons debate, in which Republicans were eager to score points against the White House on China; an examination of how Dr. Lee's handling of classified information compared with the usual practices in the laboratories; a closer look at Notra Trulock, the intelligence official at the Department of Energy who sounded some of the loudest alarms about Chinese espionage; and an exploration of the various suspects and leads that federal investigators passed up in favor of Dr. Lee.

In those instances where we fell short of our standards in our coverage of this story, the blame lies principally with those who directed the coverage, for not raising questions that occurred to us only later. Nothing in this experience undermines our faith in any of our reporters, who remained persistent and fair-minded in their newsgathering in the face of some fierce attacks.

An enormous amount remains unknown or disputed about the case of Dr. Lee and the larger issue of Chinese espionage, including why the scientist transferred classified computer code to an easily accessible computer and then tried to hide the fact (a development first reported in The Times), and how the government case evolved. Even the best investigative reporting is performed under deadline pressure, with the best assessment of information available at the time. We have dispatched a team of reporters, including the reporters who broke our first stories, to go back to the beginning of these controversies and do more reporting, drawing on sources and documents that were not previously available. Our coverage of this case is not over.

150th Anniversary: 1851-2001; Turning Away From the Holocaust

BY MAX FRANKEL | NOV. 14, 2001

AND THEN THERE WAS FAILURE: none greater than the staggering, staining failure of The New York Times to depict Hitler's methodical extermination of the Jews of Europe as a horror beyond all other horrors in World War II — a Nazi war within the war crying out for illumination.

The annihilation of six million Jews would not for many years become distinctively known as the Holocaust. But its essence became knowable fast enough, from ominous Nazi threats and undisputed eyewitness reports collected by American correspondents, agents and informants. Indeed, a large number of those reports appeared in The Times. But they were mostly buried inside its gray and stolid pages, never featured, analyzed or rendered truly comprehensible.

Yet what they printed made clear that the editors did not long mistrust the ghastly reports. They presented them as true within months of Hitler's secret resolve in 1941 to proceed to the "final solution" of his fantasized "Jewish problem."

Why, then, were the terrifying tales almost hidden in the back pages? Like most — though not all — American media, and most of official Washington, The Times drowned its reports about the fate of Jews in the flood of wartime news. Its neglect was far from unique and its reach was not then fully national, but as the premier American source of wartime news, it surely influenced the judgment of other news purveyors.

While a few publications — newspapers like The Post (then liberal) and PM in New York and magazines like The Nation and The New Republic — showed more conspicuous concern, The Times's coverage generally took the view that the atrocities inflicted upon Europe's Jews, while horrific, were not significantly different from those visited upon tens of millions of other war victims, nor more noteworthy.

SIX YEARS, SIX PAGE 1 ARTICLES

Only six times in nearly six years did The Times's front page mention Jews as Hitler's unique target for total annihilation. Only once was their fate the subject of a lead editorial. Only twice did their rescue inspire passionate cries in the Sunday magazine.

Although The Times's news columns in those years did not offer as much analysis or synthesis as they do today, the paper took great pride in ranking the importance of events each morning and in carefully reviewing the major news of every week and every year. How could it happen that the war on the Jews never qualified for such highlighted attention?

There is no surviving record of how the paper's coverage of the subject was discussed by Times editors during the war years of 1939-45. But within that coverage is recurring evidence of a guiding principle: do not feature the plight of Jews, and take care, when reporting it, to link their suffering to that of many other Europeans.

This reticence has been a subject of extensive scholarly inquiry and also much speculation and condemnation. Critics have blamed "self-hating Jews" and "anti-Zionists" among the paper's owners and staff. Defenders have cited the sketchiness of much information about the death camps in Eastern Europe and also the inability of prewar generations to fully comprehend the industrial gassing of millions of innocents — a machinery of death not yet exposed by those chilling mounds of Jews' bones, hair, shoes, rings.

No single explanation seems to suffice for what was surely the century's bitterest journalistic failure. The Times, like most media of that era, fervently embraced the wartime policies of the American and British governments, both of which strongly resisted proposals to rescue Jews or to offer them haven. After a decade of economic depression, both governments had political reasons to discourage immigration and diplomatic reasons to refuse Jewish settlements in regions like Palestine.

Then, too, papers owned by Jewish families, like The Times, were plainly afraid to have a society that was still widely anti-Semitic misread their passionate opposition to Hitler as a merely parochial cause. Even some leading Jewish groups hedged their appeals for rescue lest they be accused of wanting to divert wartime energies.

At The Times, the reluctance to highlight the systematic slaughter of Jews was also undoubtedly influenced by the views of the publisher, Arthur Hays Sulzberger. He believed strongly and publicly that Judaism was a religion, not a race or nationality — that Jews should be separate only in the way they worshiped. He thought they needed no state or political and social institutions of their own. He went to great lengths to avoid having The Times branded a "Jewish newspaper." He resented other publications for emphasizing the Jewishness of people in the news.

And it was his policy, on most questions, to steer The Times toward the centrist values of America's governmental and intellectual elites. Because his editorial page, like the American government and other leading media, refused to dwell on the Jews' singular victimization, it was cool to all measures that might have singled them out for rescue or even special attention.

Only once did The Times devote its lead editorial to the subject. That was on Dec. 2, 1942, after the State Department had unofficially confirmed to leading rabbis that two million Jews had already been slain and that five million more were indeed "in danger of extermination." Even that editorial, however, retreated quickly from any show of special concern. Insisting in its title that Jews were merely "The First to Suffer," it said the same fate awaited "people of other faiths and of many races," including "our own 'mongrel' nation" and even Hitler's allies in Japan if he were to win the war.

In only one 48-hour period, in early March 1943, was the paper moved to concede in multiple ways that Europe's Jews merited extraordinary attention. The impetus apparently came from Anne O'Hare McCormick, the foreign affairs columnist, a favorite of Sulzberger and a member of his editorial board, who thought that a Madison Square Garden rally pleading for the rescue of Jews had exposed "the shame of the world."

"There is not the slightest question," she wrote, "that the persecution of the Jews has reached its awful climax in a campaign to wipe them out of Europe. If the Christian community does not support to the utmost the belated proposal worked out to rescue the Jews remaining in Europe from the fate prepared for them, we have accepted the Hitlerian thesis and forever compromised the principles for which we are pouring out blood and wealth."

Beside her column on March 3, the last of seven editorials allowed that Hitler had condemned the Jews to death "where others are sometimes let off with slavery." Vaguely urging the United States to revise "the chilly formalism of its immigration regulations," it urged other free nations to let no "secondary considerations" bar entry of those refugees who might yet escape from the Nazis' control.

On the previous day, that same Garden rally was described in an exceptional half-page article, beginning with three paragraphs on Page 1 under the smallest of 11 front-page headlines:

SAVE DOOMED JEWS,
HUGE RALLY PLEADS

As never before or after, that day's coverage included long quotations from speeches and even the text of the rally's "resolution" calling for urgent measures to move Jews out of Hitler's grasp.

When more than a year later the editorial page returned to the subject and supported the idea of temporarily housing refugees in isolated American camps, it urged saving "innocent people" without ever using the word "Jew."

On its dense inside pages, however, The Times was much less hesitant about offering persuasive and gruesome details of the systematic murders of Jews. Hundreds of short items and scores of longer articles from different corners of Europe bore out the prophetic dispatch from the Berlin bureau that had appeared on Page 5 on Sept. 13, 1939, two weeks after Hitler invaded Poland:

NAZIS HINT PURGE
OF JEWS IN POLAND

"First intimations," it began, "that a solution of the 'Jewish problem' in Poland is on the German-Polish agenda are revealed in a 'special report' of the official German News Bureau." Given the report's claim that Polish Jewry "continually fortified and enlarged" Western Jewry, the Times correspondent added, it was hard to see how their "removal" would change things "without their extermination."

On March 1, 1942, just seven weeks after the notorious Wannsee Conference distributed orders about the mass-murder weapons to be used against Jews, an article on Page 28 bore this headline:

EXTINCTION FEARED
BY JEWS IN POLAND

Polish intellectuals and officials cited underground sources for the warning that 3.5 million Jews stood condemned "to cruel death — to complete annihilation."

By June 13, the threat became official: "Nazis Blame Jews/For Big Bombings" read a headline on Page 7. The accompanying article quoted Joseph Goebbels as vowing that the Jews would pay for German suffering "with the extermination of their race in all Europe and perhaps even beyond Europe."

Two weeks later, two paragraphs appended to the end of a related article brought the news that "probably the greatest mass slaughter in history" had already claimed the lives of 700,000 Jews in Poland — a slaughter employing "machine-gun bullets, hand grenades, gas chambers, concentration camps, whipping, torture instruments and starvation." By June 30, a brief item said the World Jewish Congress put the death toll at one million.

Still greater detail followed, on Page 6 of the July 2 issue, in a London report quoting the Polish government in exile. It cited the use of gas chambers to kill 1,000 Jews a day in different cities and the staging of a blood bath in the Warsaw ghetto. It said that "the criminal German government is fulfilling Hitler's threat that, whoever wins, all Jews will be murdered." Typically, the headline, "Allies Are Urged/To Execute Nazis," was no larger than that on a neighboring article about a Polish diplomat who died in a plunge on Riverside Drive.

EXTERMINATION ORDER ON PAGE 10

On Nov. 25, a lengthy London dispatch on Page 10 cited roundups, gassings, cattle cars and the disappearance of 90 percent of Warsaw's ghetto population. It said Heinrich Himmler, the Gestapo head, had ordered the extermination of half of Poland's Jews before the end of 1942.

That same month, the State Department finally conceded that it had confirmed the extermination campaign but insisted that the Allies were helpless to prevent it. By Dec. 9, 1942, President Franklin D. Roosevelt was reported on Page 20 to have promised Jewish petitioners eventual punishment of the Nazi murderers. He was told that "the scientific and low-cost extermination" had claimed almost two million lives. There followed a rare front-page notice, on Dec. 18, under the smallest of a dozen headlines: "11 Allies Condemn/Nazi War on Jews." A brief editorial that day observed that this protest responded not just to the outcry of victims but to "officially established facts."

For once, The Times Magazine now felt free to offer a passionate plea for Europe's Jews. A brief essay by the novelist Sholem Asch on Feb. 7, 1943, recounted "the inhuman process of transportation in sealed, unventilated, limed freight cars, which are death traps."

"Those that survive," he wrote, "become as human waste to be thrown into mass-slaughter houses."

The magazine's next and last article on the subject, by Arthur Koestler on June 9, 1944, dealt mainly with the difficulty of comprehending "the greatest mass killing in recorded history."

Yet comparable emotion appeared in The Times only in a half dozen large advertisements pleading for "ACTION — NOT PITY!" They were from groups urging the rescue of Jews or the formation of an avenging Jewish army in Palestine. Only passing notice recorded the mounting Jewish death toll: 3 million in August 1943, 4 million in July 1944, 5.5 million in November 1944.

NEVER THE LEAD ARTICLE OF THE DAY

No article about the Jews' plight ever qualified as The Times's leading story of the day, or as a major event of a week or year. The ordinary reader of its pages could hardly be blamed for failing to comprehend the enormity of the Nazis' crime.

As Laurel Leff, an assistant professor at the Northeastern School of Journalism, has concluded, it was a tragic demonstration of how "the facts didn't speak for themselves." She has been the most diligent independent student of The Times's Holocaust coverage and deftly summarized her findings last year in The Harvard International Journal of Press/Politics.

"You could have read the front page of The New York Times in 1939 and 1940," she wrote, "without knowing that millions of Jews were being sent to Poland, imprisoned in ghettos, and dying of disease and starvation by the tens of thousands. You could have read the front page in 1941 without knowing that the Nazis were machine-gunning hundreds of thousands of Jews in the Soviet Union.

"You could have read the front page in 1942 and not have known, until the last month, that the Germans were carrying out a plan to annihilate European Jewry. In 1943, you would have been told once that Jews from France, Belgium and the Netherlands were being sent to slaughterhouses in Poland and that more than half of the Jews of Europe were dead, but only in the context of a single story on a rally by Jewish groups that devoted more space to who had spoken than to who had died.

"In 1944, you would have learned from the front page of the existence of horrible places such as Maidanek and Auschwitz, but only inside the paper could you find that the victims were Jews. In 1945, [liberated] Dachau and Buchenwald were on the front page, but the Jews were buried inside."

A story buried but not, over time, forgotten.

After the Nazis' slaughter of Jews was fully exposed at war's end, Iphigene Ochs Sulzberger, the influential daughter, wife and mother of Times publishers, changed her mind about the need for a Jewish state and helped her husband, Arthur Hays Sulzberger, accept the idea of Israel and befriend its leaders. Later, led by their son, Arthur Ochs Sulzberger, and their grandson Arthur Sulzberger Jr., The Times shed its sensitivity about its Jewish roots, allowed Jews to ascend to the editor's chair and warmly supported Israel in many editorials.

And to this day the failure of America's media to fasten upon Hitler's mad atrocities stirs the conscience of succeeding generations of reporters and editors. It has made them acutely alert to ethnic barbarities in far-off places like Uganda, Rwanda, Bosnia and Kosovo. It leaves them obviously resolved that in the face of genocide, journalism shall not have failed in vain.

From the Editors; The Times and Iraq

BY THE NEW YORK TIMES | MAY 26, 2004

OVER THE LAST YEAR this newspaper has shone the bright light of hindsight on decisions that led the United States into Iraq. We have examined the failings of American and allied intelligence, especially on the issue of Iraq's weapons and possible Iraqi connections to international terrorists. We have studied the allegations of official gullibility and hype. It is past time we turned the same light on ourselves.

In doing so — reviewing hundreds of articles written during the prelude to war and into the early stages of the occupation — we found an enormous amount of journalism that we are proud of. In most cases, what we reported was an accurate reflection of the state of our knowledge at the time, much of it painstakingly extracted from intelligence agencies that were themselves dependent on sketchy information. And where those articles included incomplete information or pointed in a wrong direction, they were later overtaken by more and stronger information. That is how news coverage normally unfolds.

But we have found a number of instances of coverage that was not as rigorous as it should have been. In some cases, information that was controversial then, and seems questionable now, was insufficiently qualified or allowed to stand unchallenged. Looking back, we wish we had been more aggressive in re-examining the claims as new evidence emerged — or failed to emerge.

The problematic articles varied in authorship and subject matter, but many shared a common feature. They depended at least in part on information from a circle of Iraqi informants, defectors and exiles bent on "regime change" in Iraq, people whose credibility has come under increasing public debate in recent weeks. (The most prominent of the anti-Saddam campaigners, Ahmad Chalabi, has been named as an occasional source in Times articles since at least 1991, and has introduced reporters to other exiles. He became a favorite of hard-liners within the Bush administration and a paid broker of information from Iraqi exiles, until his payments were cut off last week.) Complicating matters for journalists, the accounts of these exiles were often eagerly confirmed by United States officials convinced of the need to intervene in Iraq. Administration officials now acknowledge that they sometimes fell for misinformation from these exile sources. So did many news organizations — in particular, this one.

Some critics of our coverage during that time have focused blame on individual reporters. Our examination, however, indicates that the problem was more complicated. Editors at several levels who should have been challenging reporters and pressing for more skepticism were perhaps too intent on rushing scoops into the paper. Accounts of Iraqi defectors were not always weighed against their strong desire to have Saddam Hussein ousted. Articles based on dire claims about Iraq tended to get prominent display, while follow-up articles that called the original ones into question were sometimes buried. In some cases, there was no follow-up at all.

On Oct. 26 and Nov. 8, 2001, for example, Page 1 articles cited Iraqi defectors who described a secret Iraqi camp where Islamic terrorists were trained and biological weapons produced. These accounts have never been independently verified.

On Dec. 20, 2001, another front-page article began, "An Iraqi defector who described himself as a civil engineer said he personally worked on renovations of secret facilities for biological, chemical and nuclear weapons in underground wells, private villas and under the Saddam Hussein Hospital in Baghdad as recently as a year ago." Knight Ridder Newspapers reported last week that American officials took that defector — his name is Adnan Ihsan Saeed al-Haideri — to Iraq earlier this year to point out the sites where he claimed to have worked, and that the officials failed to find evidence of their use for weapons programs. It is still possible that chemical or biological weapons will be unearthed in Iraq, but in this case it looks as if we, along with the administration, were taken in. And until now we have not reported that to our readers.

On Sept. 8, 2002, the lead article of the paper was headlined "U.S. Says Hussein Intensified Quest for A-Bomb Parts." That report concerned the aluminum tubes that the administration advertised insistently as components for the manufacture of nuclear weapons fuel. The claim came not from defectors but from the best American intelligence sources available at the time. Still, it should have been presented more cautiously. There were hints that the usefulness of the tubes in making nuclear fuel was not a sure thing, but the hints were buried deep, 1,700 words into a 3,600-word article. Administration officials were allowed to hold forth at length on why this evidence of Iraq's nuclear intentions demanded that Saddam Hussein be dislodged from power: "The first sign of a 'smoking gun,' they argue, may be a mushroom cloud."

Five days later, the Times reporters learned that the tubes were in fact a subject of debate among intelligence agencies. The misgivings appeared deep in an article on Page A13, under a headline that gave no inkling that we were revising our earlier view ("White House Lists Iraq Steps to Build Banned Weapons"). The Times gave voice to skeptics of the tubes on Jan. 9, when the key piece of evidence was challenged by the International Atomic Energy Agency. That challenge was reported on Page A10; it might well have belonged on Page A1.

On April 21, 2003, as American weapons-hunters followed American troops into Iraq, another front-page article declared, "Illicit Arms Kept Till Eve of War, an Iraqi Scientist Is Said to Assert." It began this way: "A scientist who claims to have worked in Iraq's chemical weapons program for more than a decade has told an American military team that Iraq destroyed chemical weapons and biological warfare equipment only days before the war began, members of the team said."

The informant also claimed that Iraq had sent unconventional weapons to Syria and had been cooperating with Al Qaeda — two claims that were then, and remain, highly controversial. But the tone of the article suggested that this Iraqi "scientist" — who in a later article described himself as an official of military intelligence — had provided the justification the Americans had been seeking for the invasion.

The Times never followed up on the veracity of this source or the attempts to verify his claims.

A sample of the coverage, including the articles mentioned here, is online at nytimes.com/critique. Readers will also find there a detailed discussion written for The New York Review of Books last month by Michael Gordon, military affairs correspondent of The Times, about the aluminum tubes report. Responding to the review's critique of Iraq coverage, his statement could serve as a primer on the complexities of such intelligence reporting.

We consider the story of Iraq's weapons, and of the pattern of misinformation, to be unfinished business. And we fully intend to continue aggressive reporting aimed at setting the record straight.

Climate Questions and Fox News

BY JOHN COLLINS RUDOLF | DEC. 17, 2010

A TOP EDITOR for Fox News Channel directed reporters last year to question the legitimacy of scientific findings showing that the planet is warming, according to an internal e-mail obtained by the media-watchdog group Media Matters.

The e-mail, which Media Matters said was written by the Fox News Washington bureau chief, Bill Sammon, was sent on Dec. 8, 2009, a day after the start of the United Nations climate change conference in Copenhagen.

"Given the controversy over the veracity of climate change data... we should refrain from asserting that the planet has warmed (or cooled) in any given period without IMMEDIATELY pointing out that such theories are based upon data that critics have called into question," Mr. Sammon wrote.

"It is not our place as journalists to assert such notions as facts, especially as this debate intensifies," the message said.

The e-mail, which Media Matters said was provided by a Fox News employee, was sent just minutes after a live report by the White House correspondent for Fox News, Wendell Goler, from Copenhagen. In the segment, Mr. Goler described a recent report by the World Meteorological Association, a United Nations organization, estimating that the years 2000 through 2009 would prove to be the warmest on record.

The United Nations analysis was based on a synthesis of temperature data from three separate organizations: NASA, the federal National Climate Data Center and a joint record by Britain's Met Office and the University of East Anglia.

All three temperature sets indicate that the planet's surface has warmed about 1.4 degrees Fahrenheit since record-keeping began. Most of the warming has been recorded in the past three decades.

In October 2009, thousands of internal e-mails from the servers of the University of East Anglia's Climate Research Unit were anonymously released online. Excerpts of the e-mails were cited by climate change skeptics and deniers to cast doubt on the veracity of the science behind global warming.

In-depth investigations by the news media in Britain and the United States determined that while the leaked e-mails cited instances of questionable behavior by scientists, they showed no evidence of scientific fraud.

"The messages don't support claims that the science of global warming was faked," the Associated Press wrote on Dec. 12, 2009, after an exhaustive review of the 1,073 e-mails by five reporters and numerous scientific experts.

In a blog post about Mr. Sammon's e-mail on his Web site, Al Gore, the former vice president, said it was "unsurprising, yet still disturbing, that Fox would allow its political bias to infiltrate its news reporting" about the Copenhagen conference.

"Fox News has consistently delivered false and misleading information to its viewers about the climate crisis. The leaked e-mails now suggest that this bias comes directly from the executives responsible for their news coverage," Mr. Gore wrote.

Fox News did not return calls or e-mails requesting comment.

Lessons in a Surveillance Drama Redux

OPINION | BY MARGARET SULLIVAN | NOV. 9, 2013

IT WAS ALMOST EIGHT YEARS AGO that The Times published a blockbuster story by James Risen and Eric Lichtblau about a secret Bush administration program to eavesdrop on Americans without warrants. But for many Times readers, it still resonates deeply.

The 13-month delay in publishing the article, a period that spanned a presidential election, continues to bother these readers. Why did The Times, at the urgent request of the administration, wait so long? What does that say about the relationship between the government and the press? Would the same thing happen today? I hear about it often in email and online comments. It crops up in newspaper columns, on Twitter, in journalism reviews.

Now, in light of the huge leak of classified information on government surveillance from Edward J. Snowden, the former contractor for the National Security Agency, the episode has a renewed currency.

Mr. Snowden has said that, because of this very episode, he chose to take his trove elsewhere (largely to Glenn Greenwald at The Guardian, to the video journalist Laura Poitras and to Barton Gellman at The Washington Post). Mr. Snowden recently told the journalist Natasha Vargas-Cooper that those who put themselves in danger to leak information "must have absolute confidence that the journalists they go to will report on that information rather than bury it."

In recent weeks, I have interviewed some of the key players in that nine-year-old drama. The episode — much written about elsewhere, in New York magazine, in The Washington Post, in a book by Mr. Lichtblau and in a new one by Peter Baker of The Times — has gone largely unexplained in the pages of The Times itself.

The public editor at that time, Byron Calame, submitted a long list of questions to Times leadership but got no answers. He later wrote

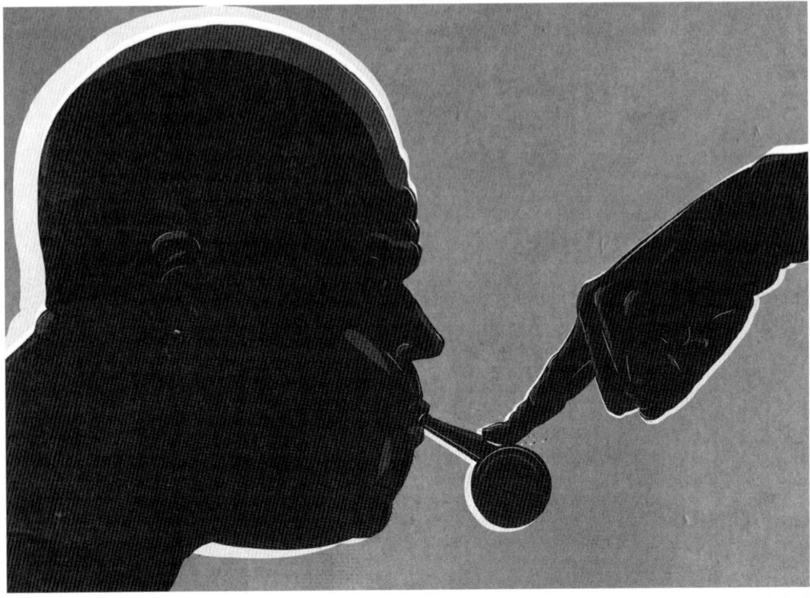

DANIEL STOLLE

about one element of the situation, establishing that the article could have appeared before the presidential election of 2004, in which George W. Bush won a second term. More recently, HBO bought the rights and had a screenplay written. Certainly, there is cinematic material here: The reporters who fought to publish; the government officials who wanted to kill the story (even arranging a last-ditch Oval Office meeting where Mr. Bush made the case to the Times publisher, Arthur Sulzberger Jr.); the big-name editors weighing the decision.

Given the episode's recent re-emergence, I thought it might be useful to examine it here, in order to give Times readers a deeper understanding of what happened and why, and to explore why it matters now and what the lessons might be.

Everyone involved sees the episode as inextricably linked with its moment in time — its proximity to 9/11 and all that followed. Some also say that a tumultuous era at The Times, after the Jayson Blair scandal and the flawed reporting in the run-up to the Iraq war, may have made editors more cautious.

"The whole confluence was pretty remarkable," Mr. Lichtblau told me. Although he strongly believed, and still does, that the story should have run when it was first ready — the fall of 2004 — he sees the historical context as a major reason that it did not.

So does Bill Keller, then the executive editor, who — on the recommendation of the Washington bureau chief at the time, Philip Taubman — decided against running the original story.

"Three years after 9/11, we, as a country, were still under the influence of that trauma, and we, as a newspaper, were not immune," Mr. Keller said. "It was not a kind of patriotic rapture. It was an acute sense that the world was a dangerous place."

Michael V. Hayden, who was the director of the N.S.A. and later the director of the Central Intelligence Agency, told me in an interview that he argued strenuously against publication, right up until the moment when The Times decided to go ahead. His rationale: "That this effort was designed to intercept threatening communication" and to prevent another terrorist attack.

In the end, The Times published the story with a couple of guns held to its head: First, the knowledge that the information in the article was also contained in a book by Mr. Risen, "State of War," whose publication date was bearing down like a freight train. Second, at the end, the word of a possible injunction against publishing, Mr. Risen said, provided a final push: "It was like a lightning bolt." (Mr. Hayden said that would not have happened: "Prior restraint was never in the cards.")

Like a game of chicken played on a high wire, it remains "the most stressful and traumatic time of my life," Mr. Risen recalls. Although The Times later said that further reporting strengthened the story enough to justify publishing it, few doubt that Mr. Risen's book was what took an essentially dead story and revived it in late 2005. "Jim's book was the driving force," Mr. Lichtblau said.

There was another important factor, he said. "The Bush administration actively misled us, claiming there was never a doubt that the wiretapping operations were legal." That turned out to be "laughably untrue." In fact, there was an imminent revolt on this very issue within the Justice Department.

What would happen now? What if Mr. Snowden had brought his information trove to The Times? By all accounts, The Times would have published the revelations — just as it did many WikiLeaks stories.

"I think our story broke the fever," Mr. Risen said. "We're much better now" about pushing back against government pressure. Jill Abramson, the executive editor (then managing editor), has not only defended the Snowden-related stories as squarely in the public interest but has had Times reporters and editors collaborating with The Guardian and ProPublica on Snowden-sourced stories.

Is it ever appropriate for the press to hold back information at the government's urging? It depends on whom you ask. Mr. Hayden would answer that one way; Mr. Greenwald quite another. (And even Mr. Hayden told me that he can't prove any harm to national security from the publication of the eavesdropping stories — then or now.) I like Mr. Risen's answer: "Very rarely."

Mr. Keller and Mr. Taubman say that they made the best decisions they could at the time, after a great deal of consideration. "If people knew everything, different people would reach different conclusions," Mr. Keller said. As for whether publishing the article in the fall of 2004 would have changed history, it's impossible to know.

"It's become an unexamined article of faith" on the left, he said, that early publication might have given John Kerry the presidency.

One thing is certain, Mr. Keller said. The story (published in December 2005, it won a Pulitzer Prize in 2006) "looks prescient," he said, adding: "We know now that people with noble intentions can run way out of bounds. Risen and Lichtblau were on to that a long time ago."

What's more, the reporters were working without the cache of classified documentation that a whistle-blower might have. They based their story on the patient development of confidential sources.

Mr. Taubman remembers his fateful recommendation not to publish as "an agonizing one." He dismisses any role played by his relationships with members of the Bush administration, including Condoleezza Rice, with whom he shares longstanding and close ties to Stanford University (where they both now teach). As national security adviser in 2004 and secretary of state in 2005, she opposed the article's publication, he said. But "that did not affect my thinking," which was that national security would be harmed by publication.

What if he knew then everything he knows now, in light of the Snowden revelations? "I would have made a different decision had I known that Jim and Eric were tugging on a thread that led to a whole tapestry," Mr. Taubman said.

Given the law of unintended consequences, and a fair helping of irony, the publication of the warrantless eavesdropping story resonates now in quite another way: The furor it caused prompted the Bush administration to push hard for changes in the laws governing surveillance.

"Our story set in motion the process of making all this stuff legal," Mr. Lichtblau said. "Now it's all encoded in law. Bush got everything he wanted on his way out of office."

There may be public outrage over the latest wave of surveillance revelations, but the government has a helpful defense: Hey, it's legal.

Mr. Taubman now teaches a course at Stanford — titled "Need to Know" — about the tension between government and the news media. He recently brought Mr. Hayden in as a guest speaker.

What is the major lesson, then, of the drama in which Mr. Taubman played such a crucial role?

"The old adage, which we violated, is still a good one," he said. "Always err on the side of publishing."

MARGARET SULLIVAN is the fifth public editor appointed by The New York Times.

Why Readers See The Times as Liberal

OPINION | BY LIZ SPAYD | JULY 23, 2016

I HAVE BEEN HERE less than a month, but already I've discovered something that surely must be bad for business if your business is running The New York Times. It comes via the inbox to the public editor, from people like Gary Taustine of Manhattan, who writes: "The NY Times is alienating its independent and open-minded readers, and in doing so, limiting the reach of their message and its possible influence."

One reader from California who asked not to be named believes Times reporters and editors are trying to sway public opinion toward their own beliefs. "I never thought I'd see the day when I, as a liberal, would start getting so frustrated with the one-sided reporting that I would start hopping over to the Fox News webpage to read an article and get the rest of the story that the NYT refused to publish," she says.

Here's frustration as it crests, from James, an Arizona reader: "You've lost a subscriber because of your relentless bias against Trump — and I'm not even a Republican."

You can imagine what the letters from actual conservatives sound like.

Emails like these stream into this office every day. A perception that The Times is biased prompts some of the most frequent complaints from readers. Only they arrive so frequently, and have for so long, that the objections no longer land with much heft.

Like the tiresome bore at a party, I went around asking several journalists in the newsroom about these claims that The Times sways to the left. Mostly I was met with a roll of the eyes. All sides hate us, they said. We're tough on everyone. That's nothing new here.

That response may be tempting, but unless the strategy is to become The New Republic gone daily, this perception by many readers strikes me as poison. A paper whose journalism appeals to only half the country has a dangerously severed public mission. And a news organization trying to survive off revenue from readers shouldn't erase American conservatives from its list of prospects.

No one here would tell me the ideological breakdown of The Times's total audience or subscriber base, numbers that are considered proprietary. I know only that there is unease in at least a few offices about whether The Times feels sufficiently relevant to a broad slice of readers.

Why is it that conservatives, and even many moderates, see in The Times a blue-state worldview? Let's set aside for now the core of their criticism — that the coverage is in fact biased. I'll be turning to that as I settle into the job. My focus here is only on the perceptions. Because while one might debate the substance of the claims, the building blocks that created them are in plain sight.

The home page is a good place to start. Anchoring its top right corner is the Opinion section, which promotes the columns and editorials of its mostly liberal writers. "Readers know the difference between opinion and news," you'll often hear. I'm not so sure all do, especially when the website makes neighbors of the two and social platforms make them nearly impossible to tease apart.

Maybe we're well past worrying about that. So turn to the drumbeat of Hillary Clinton campaign ads on the website. Even for me, who fully knows an ad from a news story, seeing Clinton's smiling face when I've come to read the news can be rather jarring.

Readers often run across ads like these on The New York Times's homepage.

How about all the reader comments attached to political articles? On most days, conservatives occupy just a few back-row seats in this giant liberal echo chamber, not because Republicans are screened out by editors but because they don't show up in the first place. Bassey Etim, who oversees the comments forum, makes a point of salting conservative voices into the week's list of top commenters. "It just makes the conversation more dynamic and interesting," he says.

For some print readers, the placement of an editorial calling for gun control on the front page last December, which garnered a record number of comments, was shrill proof of the kind of Times bias they expect. There was a torrent of debate over the appropriateness of its placement.

I asked Dean Baquet, the executive editor, about the perception of liberal bias that hangs over his newsroom, whether from the gun editorial, the Clinton ads, or the actual work of his journalists. He doesn't believe that the coverage on most days has a liberal cast, nor does he think campaign ads or the rare front-page editorial create that perception.

But he does want The Times's reach to be wide. "We have to be really careful that people feel like they can see themselves in The New York Times," he said. "I want us to be perceived as fair and honest to the world, not just a segment of it. It's a really difficult goal. Do we pull it off all the time? No."

I agree with Baquet: It isn't easy. But it's not hard to imagine some small steps on a longer journey — leaving editorials on the editorial page, banning campaign ads from the home page, or building a better mix of values into the ranks of the newsroom's urban progressives.

That last one might even help reporting between the country's coastlines, where the trust level can be gaping. Mark Leibovich, a veteran political writer on the magazine staff whose job entails talking to voters across the spectrum, believes The Times's coverage is generally balanced. But the perception that it isn't complicates his job. "It's becoming a much more menacing factor," he said. "You get hit with complaints that we're biased pretty much whenever you go out, especially at a Republican rally."

What's happening at The Times isn't only about The Times. It's part of a fracturing media environment that reflects a fractured country. That in turn leads liberals and conservatives toward separate news sources. A Pew Research Center survey two years ago found that liberals are flocking to The Times, with 65 percent of its readers possessing political values that were left of center.

Does that mean The Times should write off conservatives and make a hard play for the left and perhaps center left? I hope that question is not on the table. It would change everything about what the paper is and the force of its journalism.

Imagine what would be missed by journalists who felt no pressing need to see the world through others' eyes. Imagine the stories they might miss, like the groundswell of isolation that propelled a candidate like Donald Trump to his party's nomination. Imagine a country where the greatest, most powerful newsroom in the free world was viewed not as a voice that speaks to all but as one that has taken sides.

Or has that already happened?

LIZ SPAYD is the sixth public editor appointed by The New York Times. She evaluates journalistic integrity and examines both the quality of the journalism and the standards being applied across the newsroom. She writes a regular column expressing her views. The public editor works outside of the reporting and editing structure of the newsroom and receives and answers questions or comments from readers and the public, principally about news and other coverage in The Times. Her opinions and conclusions are her own.

Former Fox News Analyst Calls Network a 'Destructive Propaganda Machine'

BY MATTHEW HAAG | JUNE 7, 2018

FOR 10 YEARS, Ralph Peters regularly appeared on Fox News to offer military analysis and insight as one of the cable network's reliably conservative commenters. But he quit in March in disgust.

Mr. Peters, who announced his departure in a blistering farewell note to his colleagues, followed up on Wednesday with another searing attack, saying that the network was "doing a great, grave disservice to our country."

The retired lieutenant colonel in the United States Army spoke on CNN in his first television interview since his departure. "With the rise of Donald Trump, Fox did become a destructive propaganda machine," Mr. Peters said. "And I don't do propaganda for anyone."

For the decade he worked there, Mr. Peters said he believed that Fox News was a necessary and legitimate conservative bulwark in the news media and an outlet for libertarian opinions. But under President Trump, the network shifted rightward, he said.

Its popular prime time hosts, particularly Sean Hannity, started to echo Mr. Trump's debunked theories of a "deep state" undermining his administration. They joined the president in steadily attacking the Justice Department, the F.B.I. and other democratic institutions, Mr. Peters said.

"I suspect Sean Hannity really believes it," he said. "The others are smarter. They know what they're doing. It's bewildering to me. I mean, I wanted to just cry out and say: 'How can you do this? How can you lie to our country?' "

On Thursday morning, Alisyn Camerota, a former Fox News anchor who now works at CNN, said that Mr. Peters's remarks mirrored her own experience at the network.

"I too was upset about the blurring of the lines between propaganda and journalism," Ms. Camerota said after a clip of his remarks was played. "I don't know whether the viewers know the difference between the prime time hosts and the great reporters there."

Fox News said Thursday that it stood by its statement from when Mr. Peters departed in March. "Ralph Peters is entitled to his opinion despite the fact that he's choosing to use it as a weapon in order to gain attention," the network said then. "We are extremely proud of our top-rated prime time hosts and all of our opinion programing."

Fox News and Mr. Trump enjoy a symbiotic relationship. He is a loyal viewer of its morning program "Fox & Friends," often tweeting about what the hosts discuss and sometimes calling in for lengthy interviews. At night, a lineup of opinion shows offers a friendly space for Trump supporters. The friendliest might be "Hannity," whose host is also an influential Trump confidant.

Mr. Hannity, as well as reporters and anchors from the network's news division, are traveling to Singapore for Mr. Trump's June 12 summit meeting with North Korea's leader, Kim Jong-un. "Hannity" will be broadcast live for three nights in Singapore, the network said.

The Six Forms of Media Bias

OPINION | BY DAVID LEONHARDT | JAN. 31, 2019

A media critic inveighs against the bias toward centrism, which inspires me to come up with my own list.

"IMPARTIALITY IS STILL a value worth defending in mainstream news coverage," writes Margaret Sullivan, the Washington Post media critic. "But you don't get there by walking down the center line with a blindfold on."

Her column is a cri de coeur against the media's bias toward centrism. Too often, journalists confuse centrism with fairness, objectivity or common-sense truth. But centrism is none of those. It is a point of view, and it can be wrong, just as conservatism or liberalism can be.

Centrists were wrong about the urgency of reducing the deficit over the past decade. They were wrong about the Iraq war in 2003, wrong about the economic might of Japan in the 1980s and wrong about the economic might of the Soviet Union before that.

I'm obviously a fan — and a member — of the media. It's vital to democracy and has performed admirably in the age of Trump. But I also believe in reflection and criticism. So Sullivan's column inspired me to make a list of the biggest forms of media bias.

I came up with six. Some overlap. Others conflict — because different pieces of journalism can make different mistakes. Here goes ...

THE LIST

• **Centrist bias.** In her column, Sullivan inveighs against the bias toward political centrism and notes that it often crowds out thought-provoking political views on both the left and right. She also calls out a related problem, bothsidesism: blaming the parties equally, even when they don't deserve equal blame.

Brian Fallon, the Democratic strategist, recently had a pointed description of bothsidesism. He described it as a "a performative effort to triangulate so as to present the journalist as more deserving of the public's trust than their elected leaders. It's a political act, and shows just as much bias as picking a side."

• **Affluent bias.** The media isn't just biased toward the center. It often confuses the center with views that are actually those of the affluent. My newsletter on Tuesday — about Howard Schultz — made the fuller version of the argument.

Why does this bias exist? National journalists, the ones who often set the agenda, spend a fair amount of time around wealthy people, and national journalists themselves tend to be more affluent than most Americans. A classic example: At a 2008 Democratic primary debate, a then-anchor at ABC News anchor, Charlie Gibson, suggested that a middle class family in New Hampshire might make $200,000 a year. The audience laughed.

• **Bias for the new.** Journalists often confuse newness with importance. The problem lurks in the product's name: "News." Too often, we emphasize relatively trivial stories — like candidates taking verbal swipes at each other — over more important ones, like the candidates' tax policy, as New York University's Jay Rosen has argued. In the 2016 presidential debates, for instance, the moderators almost completely ignored climate change.

• **The same biases that afflict society.** From sexism in political reporting ("likability") to racism in crime coverage (the "crack baby" stereotype), the media often suffers from the same biases that other Americans do. But we could certainly be doing more to fight back. Female and nonwhite voices remain underrepresented at major publications.

• **Liberal bias.** Yes, it's real. Most mainstream journalists do lean left.

Political reporters and Washington reporters are usually professional enough to keep these views from affecting their coverage. Instead, they're more likely to suffer from bothsidesism, even when a both-sides story isn't the most accurate one. The coverage of Hillary Clinton's emails, to take one example, certainly didn't suffer from liberal bias.

But on issue-based coverage, liberal bias exists. Education reform — the media's frequent hostility toward charter schools — is one example. My colleague Ross Douthat makes his case about liberal bias on this week's episode of "The Argument" podcast. As you will hear, I partly agreed with him and partly pushed back. Michelle Goldberg disagreed with him more fully. It was a good debate.

• **Conservative bias.** It's real, too. Fox News and talk radio are huge, influential parts of the media. They skew hard right, and they often present their readers with misleading or outright false information, be it "birtherism" or conspiracy theories.

Much of the media — local and national, news reporters and opinion columnists — tries hard to tell stories accurately and corrects itself when it errs. Fox and a lot of talk radio do not. And I'll take a fallible, self-reflective media, even with all of the biases I've listed here, over a media that is more akin to propaganda.

DAVID LEONHARDT is a former Washington bureau chief for the Times, and was the founding editor of The Upshot and head of The 2020 Project, on the future of the Times newsroom. He won the 2011 Pulitzer Prize for commentary, for columns on the financial crisis.

After Mueller Report, News Media Leaders Defend Their Work

BY AMY CHOZICK | MARCH 25, 2019

THERE HAVE BEEN tipping points and bombshells, walls closing in and turning points. And there have been so, so many declarations of "The beginning of the end!" that the comedian John Oliver had a recurring, satirical "We got him!" segment on his late-night HBO show, complete with a jubilant marching band and sequined majorettes celebrating President Trump's downfall.

But in the swirl of reporting and speculation about the 45th president, nothing has held viewers on the edge of their seats quite like the special counsel, Robert S. Mueller III, and his investigation into possible ties between Mr. Trump's 2016 campaign and Russian agents.

The story line had it all: Cold War-era intrigue, allegations of shadowy meetings in Moscow and a cast of recurring characters that included an aide in a $15,000 ostrich skin jacket (Paul D. Manafort) and another who has a tattoo of Richard Nixon on his back (Roger Stone).

Mr. Mueller's complete report hasn't yet been released, but on Sunday, Attorney General William P. Barr made public a four-page letter to Congress reporting that the 22-month inquiry did not have sufficient evidence to conclude that Mr. Trump and his associates "conspired or coordinated with the Russian government" ahead of the 2016 election. The news blindsided many liberals — particularly those with an ambient knowledge of Rachel Maddow's nightly monologues on MSNBC.

Who could blame them? The news media's coverage of the investigation, particularly on cable TV, caused millions of Americans who disapprove of Mr. Trump to put their faith in Mr. Mueller. There were even prayer candles, key chains and paintings made in the likeness of the silent 74-year-old Marine veteran, and his fans believed his looming report would bring, in the words of the "Bachelor" creator Mike Fleiss, "the most dramatic finale of a presidency ever!"

When that didn't happen, Mr. Trump and his allies placed blame on the news media for its ravenous coverage. "I think Democrats and the liberal media owe the president and they owe the American people an apology," the White House press secretary, Sarah Huckabee Sanders, said on NBC News's Today.

Rich Lowry, the editor of the conservative National Review, wrote on Twitter, "The 3 biggest losers from the Mueller report in order — the media, the media, the media."

It was a bipartisan ripping. Matt Taibbi, a Rolling Stone writer whose book on the 2016 election is titled "Insane Clown President," is not exactly a fan of Mr. Trump. And yet he called the apparent lack of new charges resulting from the special counsel's investigation "a death blow for the reputation of the American news media." He compared it to the erroneous reporting on weapons of mass destruction in the run-up to the Iraq war.

Hogan Gidley, a White House spokesman, said that, by his count, The New York Times, The Washington Post, CNN and MSNBC had published a combined 8,500 stories on the Russia probe. He specifically pointed to CNN and chyrons that would include the phrase "amid Russia investigation," no matter what the topic.

"It's so painfully obvious they wanted it to be true so badly, and the last two years of their lives and two years of their news coverage has been an entire waste," Mr. Gidley said.

Jeff Zucker, president of CNN, said he was "entirely comfortable" with the network's coverage.

"We are not investigators. We are journalists, and our role is to report the facts as we know them, which is exactly what we did," Mr. Zucker said in an email. "A sitting president's own Justice Department investigated his campaign for collusion with a hostile nation. That's not enormous because the media says so. That's enormous because it's unprecedented."

Bill Grueskin, a professor at the Columbia School of Journalism, said there seemed to be some confusion about the role of journalists.

"Mueller and Barr need to prove beyond a reasonable doubt — do we file charges or don't we?" he said. "Journalists don't have that standard."

In other words, Pulitzer Prize-winning reports of alleged wrongdoing do not need to provide evidence of criminality in order to be factual, newsworthy and relevant to readers.

"The special counsel investigation documented, as we reported, extensive Russian interference in the 2016 election and widespread deceit on the part of certain advisers to the president about Russian contacts and other matters," said Martin Baron, executive editor of The Washington Post. "Our job is to bring facts to light. Others make determinations about prosecutable criminal offenses."

Dean Baquet, the executive editor of The Times, echoed that sentiment. "We wrote a lot about Russia, and I have no regrets," he said. "It's not our job to determine whether or not there was illegality."

But in the nearly two years of the Russia investigation, there have been several high-profile mea culpas.

ABC News apologized and parted ways with its chief investigative correspondent, Brian Ross, after an errant report that Michael T. Flynn, the former national security adviser, had been directed by Mr. Trump to make contact with Russian officials during the 2016 campaign. Three seasoned investigative journalists at CNN resigned after the network retracted a report that a close Trump aide had ties to a Russian investment firm. Mr. Mueller publicly rebuked a BuzzFeed News account that Mr. Trump had instructed his longtime lawyer Michael D. Cohen to lie in his testimony to Congress. (BuzzFeed News stood by its reporting.)

"It's pretty clear that a lot of people in the media, particularly on cable news, got ahead of their skis on this," said Michael Isikoff, a co-author of "Russian Roulette: The Inside Story of Putin's War on America and the Election of Donald Trump."

Ben Smith, the editor in chief of BuzzFeed News, defended coverage of the Russian investigation, including the decision to publish a dossier put together by British intelligence officer Christopher Steele full of tantalizing (and unsubstantiated) reports about Russian efforts to blackmail Mr. Trump.

"It's pretty hard to imagine a scenario in which people were aware of its existence but not allowed to see it," Mr. Smith said of the dossier.

The editor also expressed concern that journalism was so often churned — and reduced — through the filter of partisan punditry.

"I think it's a moment when the public conversation favors partisans who are totally convinced in the rightness of what they're saying and doesn't favor reporters who are cautious about what they know and are trying to get things right," Mr. Smith said.

That may be true, but in the current ecosystem of political news, when shoe-leather reporters moonlight as cable news analysts, it can be hard for typical viewers to distinguish the pundits from the press.

Even if more damning findings come out in the full report, Mr. Trump has already cast the narrative that he is absolved and that the "fake news" media is to be blamed, said Kevin Madden, a Republican strategist and former adviser to Mitt Romney.

"You see the president's most vocal supporters, they're touting the headlines that the president was exonerated and vindicated and where are the apologies from the media?" he said.

Those apologies aren't likely to come, as long as the same people who have been trying to erode trust in factual reporting are now ones demanding a reckoning.

"We will hold every fake news media liar member accountable," Sean Hannity wrote Sunday on Twitter.

Mr. Fleiss, the producer, who knew Mr. Trump in his "Apprentice" years, said cable news had taken a page from the president's reality TV playbook in teasing every development in the Russia investigation as if it were the final blow.

"He's a master exaggerator, been doing it his entire life," Mr. Fleiss said. "The rookies tried to keep up and got burned."

CHAPTER 4

The Business of Journalism in the 21st Century

As journalism moves further into the 21st century, newspapers must adapt to the changing relationship between news and the public. While it is rooted in journalism, the industry of digital media is turbulent and changing swiftly, and the demand for rapid content generation has made for an increasingly competitive environment. Though statistics show the demand for news has never been higher, significant layoffs at media companies in January 2019 indicated a major restructuring of the industry of digital journalism.

Putting a Price on Words

BY ANDREW RICE | MAY 12, 2010

LAST YEAR, SAM APPLE got the idea into his head that what the world needed was a new kind of newspaper. This was, to put it mildly, at odds with the consensus of the marketplace. At the time, several large media companies were in bankruptcy, others were trading at penny-stock levels and analysts were seriously asking whether some venerable publications — including this one — might soon cease to exist. The recession was only worsening a fundamental problem: the industry's physical product, printed paper, was going the way of the rotary phone, and no one had yet figured out how to generate comparable revenues online. But Apple, a 34-year-old writer, wasn't ready to give up on journalism as a profit-making enterprise. He began telling friends about his plans to start a Web publication called The Faster Times.

Apple quit his part-time gig as director of interactive media for the Web site Nerve.com in New York and began recruiting. It wasn't hard to find people eager to join. Employment in New York's publishing sector shrank by a tenth last year, leaving behind a mass of glum, jobless writers. The good news, though, was that one of the very forces that was sapping industry profits — the Web's demolition of barriers to entry — also made it quite simple and cheap for anyone to become a journalism entrepreneur. Using open-source software, which Apple hired programmers to customize, The Faster Times could get up and running for less than $20,000.

Before the site went live last summer, Apple and a group of editors held marathon meetings at a Brooklyn coffee shop with free wireless Internet. In one sense, The Faster Times was supposed to be a traditional publication, staffed by trained journalists covering a wide range of beats and guided by a coherent editorial mission. Where Apple's model departed from convention, as a matter of necessity, was in the area of compensation. He couldn't afford to offer salaries and benefits, or even flat freelance fees, so instead he promised contributors 75 percent of the revenues from all advertisements placed next to their articles. Payments would start small, but if The Faster Times prospered, as Apple hoped, so would its writers. He referred to the publication as a journalistic "collective," but in truth it was a small experiment in capitalistic incentives: contributors would profit directly from their work, according to the market's assessment of its value.

And therein lies the catch — for The Faster Times, for many similar start-ups and for the entire industry of media, old and new. No one seems to know how to value the product anymore. This isn't a lament about declining standards of quality or the rude incursions of amateur bloggers. In fact, thanks to the Internet, people probably read more good journalism than ever. That's precisely the problem: the sheer volume of words has overwhelmed a business model that was once based on scarcity and limited choice.

For many years, newspapers and magazines operated in fairly uniform fashion, supported by two streams of revenue. The consumers purchased the product, and businesses paid to reach them with advertisements. Recessions came and went, ad pages expanded and contracted, publications started and went under — but nothing disturbed the basic model. Online economics have changed both sides of the profit equation. "It's dawning on people that the marketplace will no longer pay the freight," says Ken Doctor, a former newspaper executive and the author of "Newsonomics: Twelve New Trends That Will Shape the News You Get."

Early on, almost all print publications decided to offer free access to their online content, which over time cut into their print circulation. In theory, the industry should have been able to absorb the gradual loss of paying readers. Advertising always accounted for the vast majority of the publishers' revenues — with newspapers, 80 percent was the rule of thumb — and because publications could reach vastly larger audiences online, it seemed reasonable to expect that they'd be able to make more money from ads. But instead, online ads sell at rates that are a fraction of those for print, for simple reasons of competition. "In a print world you had pretty much a limited amount of inventory — pages in a magazine," says Domenic Venuto, managing director of the online marketing firm Razorfish. "In the online world, inventory has become infinite."

"Maybe this is what success looks like," says Nick Denton, speaking of his own business, Gawker Media — a popular and profitable network of Web sites covering technology, sports and celebrity news — as well as of disruptive ventures like Craigslist, the free site that has decimated classified advertising, once a lucrative source of income for newspapers. "You can have destroyed hundreds of millions of dollars, or billions of dollars, of revenue for other people," Denton says, "but without capturing it all yourself."

Yet for some — possibly foolhardy — reason, a lot of people still want to work in journalism, and even amid the depths of the recession, there have been stirrings of creativity. A multitude of younger, nimbler enterprises have popped up, unencumbered by the past and ready to try anything. History suggests that few of these ventures will ultimately survive: Web start-ups have a failure rate between 70 and 90 percent. But it's quite possible that the experiments they're staging are already producing the kind of innovations that make for new, sustainable business models.

The Faster Times went online last July, with a blast of publicity and a triumphant party in a Manhattan bookstore. The site had enlisted correspondents in 20 countries, and beats devoted to science, food, travel and the arts, in addition to goofier subjects, like time travel and jet packs. The whimsy aside, Sam Apple took his task seriously. "The crisis of American journalism," he wrote in the mission statement, is "a financial crisis. Opinions posted on blogs are cheap. Great journalism is expensive."

With any luck, he was about to discover it was also worth something.

YOU CAN'T CALL it a dot-com boom — there is not much capital, there are no parties with catered sushi and no one is expecting to get rich. But this generation of start-ups does share at least one trait with its 1990s predecessors: a conviction that they're the vanguard of an unfolding revolution. One morning, as a March gale howled down Broadway, I visited the editors of the Web site True/Slant. Their loftlike office, in a vintage SoHo building, was bare, white and slightly chilly, as if designed to reflect the present ethic of austerity. With just five employees, True/Slant has built a significant audience since it started last year: about a million readers visit the site at least once a month, a number similar to the online following of The Village Voice or The Charlotte Observer. The site owes its modest but growing success to the work of more than 300 part-time contributors. It's not so much a unified publication as a loosely connected commune of bloggers, who generate a continual stream of content with minimal editorial intervention. The company calls what it is doing "entrepreneurial journalism" and says it's the future of the profession.

True/Slant is the creation of a lean, gray-bearded 57-year-old named Lewis Dvorkin. He began his career working at newspapers and magazines, and peppers his conversation with references to sainted editors of an earlier era. "I'm old enough to be a bit of a bridge from that world to whatever world we're in today," he told me. Dvorkin's more recent and pertinent experience, however, came as a content-programming executive at AOL, where he played a role in creating the celebrity gossip site TMZ, which has since developed one of the largest audiences on the Web. A few years ago, he started toying with the idea that eventually led to True/Slant: could technology allow you to create a news organization without any of the familiar editorial hierarchies?

At True/Slant, Dvorkin told me, "you are the sole producer, creator, programmer of your content. That reduces — and this is key — the cost structure." He started the site with a modest $3 million investment from Fuse Capital and Forbes Media, picking its name off a list of compound words that were made up by a Web developer. All of True/Slant's writers are freelancers and are paid a pittance relative to the salaries offered at established media organizations. "Newsrooms today are high-cost, inefficient content-creation operations that will not be supported by advertising revenues in the digital world," Dvorkin said. "It just won't happen."

Online, advertisers have immense power. Because it's easy to track who is clicking what, they can aim with efficiency and typically pay according to the number of times their ads are actually viewed. Instead of sending word of its shoe sale to a million print newspaper subscribers, who may or may not be looking for shoes, a store can buy the page views of 50,000 people who are reading articles about fashion. Or the advertiser can place ads on heavily trafficked portal sites like Yahoo and AOL, both of which are currently expanding their production of original journalism. Or it can pay Google to insert its ads into search results. Or it can go to one of the large digital advertising networks that have arisen in recent years and buy unsold "remnant" page views at deep discounts. There is a lot less waste and a lot more choice, and the upshot is that advertising, which once produced robust margins for publishers, now sells for spare change online. Generally speaking, while some ad placements — like those on a site's home page — go for a significant premium, pages of individual articles, if sold at the going rates, bring in between a penny and nickel each time a reader looks at one.

That's not to say that it's impossible to make money. If True/Slant can keep its production costs low and its traffic high, it can collect those pennies and nickels on a scale large enough to turn a profit. There are a couple of ways to do this as an online publisher. You can emphasize quality, producing a limited number of items in the hope that each will attract a great number of readers. Or a publisher can go for quantity, producing a lot of little things that add up in the aggregate. True/Slant's low-cost newsroom churns out around 125 pieces of content a day.

Many companies practice this strategy at even higher volume. For instance, Examiner.com, owned by the billionaire Philip Anschutz, has a gigantic audience and a nationwide army of 36,000 localized contributors, or "examiners," who produce articles on subjects like community news, lifestyle issues and pets, and are paid about 1 cent per page view. AOL is trying a similar "citizen journalism" approach on a site called Patch. Probably the most successful example is the Huffington Post, which employs 70 salaried editorial staff members and 6,000 uncompensated bloggers and recently pushed into the nation's top 10 current-affairs Web sites, according to Nielsen Online, vaulting past sources like The Washington Post. The Huffington Post generates an average of 500 items a day, many of them aggregated content from other sources, and Examiner.com, more than 3,000.

Increasingly the online audience for these sites is coming in side doors, via links on blogs and social-networking Web sites like Facebook. Probably the most important tool for reaching large audiences, however, is Google. If you can climb to the top of the site's search results, you're certain to be rewarded with a huge number of clicks. Most publications these days try to harness the Google algorithm through an arcane process known as search-engine optimization. Some are more skilled at this than others. That's why, as I write in mid-April, a search for the phrase "Eyjafjallajokull Volcano" brings up a Huffington Post photo slide show near the top of its results.

A handful of enterprising new sites, like Associated Content and Demand Media, are now turning the whole process around, generating content that is specifically designed to feed Google's appetites. They don't call what they do journalism or care about breaking news, but they say they're generating huge advertising revenues, and their strategies are being closely watched. "We realized that there was this massive opportunity, that the economics of content and media distribution had shifted, and they had shifted permanently," says Steven Kydd, who oversees original content production for Demand Media. The company claims to have raked in $200 million in revenue last year and is now reportedly talking to Goldman Sachs about underwriting an initial public offering.

Demand's business model draws on the skills of thousands of freelance contributors, who pick the topics they address from an automated list of more than 200,000 written and video assignments culled from Internet search requests. The topics are mostly geared toward answering practical questions and are posted to low-profile Web sites like eHow, or to YouTube, with which Demand has a profit-sharing agreement. The company claims to have devised an algorithm that projects precisely how much advertising revenue each assignment will return. It says these mathematically generated ideas are 4.9 times as valuable as those devised by mere human brainstorming.

"Our editors absolutely love this, because they are able to sift through millions of potential titles, and they know that they are all good ideas," Kydd says. And profitable ones — nothing is assigned unless the algorithm predicts it can cover the costs of production. Demand's freelancers can make around $15 or $20 per item. "The funny part is, sometimes we'll ask people who work, say, in newspapers or magazines, 'How much did that article cost you?' " Kydd says. "They literally have no idea."

That's changing. Though journalists tend to shudder at Demand Media's approach, mainstream publishers are starting to co-opt portions of its model. USA Today, for instance, has contracted Demand to supply the content for its Travel Tips Web page, while AOL recently started a Web site called Seed, edited by Saul Hansell, a former New York Times columnist, which generates story ideas from search data. More generally, there is a growing appreciation among those who practice journalism of the Internet's capacity to tell them what readers want to know.

"For traditional journalists, this is a difficult concept for them to grasp, and one reason it's difficult is because it's scary — it's scary to actually have that data in front of you," Dvorkin said. "It's scary to say, wow, this is the audience, and now all of a sudden I have to respond to the audience because this is what they're interested in."

Dvorkin and Coates Bateman, a former book editor who runs True/Slant's daily content operations, showed me around the site's "dashboard," the back office of its virtual newsroom. There was a dial, like a digital speedometer, which showed the volume of page views on the site and a list of trending topics on Google and Twitter, topped by the confection of the moment, the teenage-pop sensation Justin Bieber. (Sure enough, within an hour or so, a Bieber-related True/Slant post appeared.) There was a list that ranked the most-viewed items and metrics that tracked how they got their traffic — maybe via a link from a popular blogger, or the recommendation tool Digg. Most eerily, there was a little algorithm-driven display that showed contributors what other people were saying about their work out in the blogosphere — eavesdropping, in real time.

True/Slant structures its compensation to give writers an incentive to hustle for readers' attention. Contributors are paid a monthly retainer and scaled bonuses based on how many people read their articles. The money isn't enough to live off — the entrepreneurial journalist has many gigs — but True/Slant is reasonably generous in comparison with, say, the Huffington Post, which pays its nonstaff bloggers nothing but esteem. Most writers make a few hundred dollars a month if they hit their traffic targets, and a few big names, like the professional controversialist Matt Taibbi, make quite a bit more. In fact, if you break it down, True/Slant pays its writers more than the amount of revenue their work generates at the current online advertising rates. Stripped down as it is, the start-up isn't yet turning a profit, and it's now in the process of raising a second round of venture capital.

I asked Bateman, as a matter of raw economics, how much an individual article is worth to True/Slant's bottom line, on average. He told me he calculated it out: around $10.

SAM APPLE AND I were sitting in a hushed and crowded cafe, amid the soft glow of open laptops. "I thought at the beginning that if I could create a top-notch journalistic outlet, and if I could do that at a small fraction of the cost, maybe advertising could cover it," he told me. The Faster Times was now eight months old, and Apple was wiser about online economics. The summer before, the site charged out of the gate with a 24-hour posting schedule, a large and enthusiastic staff and guest posts from famous writers like Gary Shteyngart. By the fall, it had acquired a monthly audience of around 200,000 readers, according to the tracking site Quantcast — small compared with the Huffington Post's but a pretty impressive return on $20,000, in Apple's opinion. But the revenues that were coming in from Google AdSense, the ad-placement service he was originally using, were so paltry that Apple wondered, when he gave writers their 75 percent share, whether he was actually driving them away.

"I have a friend who is a behavioral economist," he said. "He says that if you pay people tiny amounts, it's worse than not paying them at all." The Faster Times's first round of payments ranged from $5 to $75. Revenues have increased substantially since Apple switched to another ad service, but the writers' shares still don't amount to much. Whether it was because of that, or fickleness, or the attractions of better-paying opportunities, many of the original Faster Times contributors gradually drifted off. Apple was now trying to hatch ideas for alternate sources of revenue, to ease the site's dependence on advertising. "I still feel like there's a lot to try," Apple told me. "We can kind of be a testing ground for the latest experiments."

Many other publications, confronted with the painful math, have reached the same conclusion: the business needs alternate schemes of support. Some have adapted tried-and-true formulas. The Daily Beast is backed by a generous billionaire, Barry Diller; others are mimicking NPR's nonprofit model; Politico makes the majority of its revenue from, of all things, advertising in an offshoot print newspaper. Most familiar of all, there's the subscription route, which the online editions of The Wall Street Journal and The Financial Times have followed with success. The New York Times has announced that early next year it will institute a fee for frequent users of its site. Many analysts are doubtful that the subscription approach will work for everyone — surveys suggest that few consumers are willing to pay for news online. But some start-ups are experimenting with a variation on the idea, premium memberships, which give readers who sign up special access and perks. GlobalPost, an online publication for international news, is currently implementing such a program, offering subscribers the chance to participate in conference-call briefings by freelance correspondents stationed in more than 50 countries, and to vote on articles they'd like to see assigned.

One thing many of these new strategies have in common is a willingness to transgress time-honored barriers — for instance, by blurring the division between reporting and advertising. True/Slant offers to let advertisers use the same blogging tools that contributors do, to produce content that, while labeled, is blended into the rest of the site. Such marketing deals are central to the company's plans for future revenue growth. "Everywhere I go the whole notion of enabling marketers to create content on a news platform is well received," Lewis Dvorkin says. "It's the way the world is moving."

Not long ago, such an idea would have been considered heretical, and in many newsrooms, it still is. But clearly, attitudes are shifting. "Hopefully we're breaking down the silliness of how church and state was historically implemented," says Merrill Brown, a veteran media executive and investor who is currently building a network of local news sites. Once, most journalists took a posture of willful ignorance when it came to the economics of the industry: they never wanted to sully themselves by knowing the business. The recession has, through fear and necessity, made capitalists out of everyone.

THE NEW JOURNALISTIC entrepreneurs fall into two distinct categories. There are the proprietors, people like Charles M. Sennott, a foreign correspondent who took a Boston Globe buyout and became a founder and an executive editor of GlobalPost, or Alex Balk, Choire Sicha and David Cho, who were cut loose by Radar, a dying magazine, and decided to start the Awl, a smart and idiosyncratic commentary site. Then there are the small-scale entrepreneurs, the journalists who, having found themselves dislodged from a salaried way of living, are now scrambling to piece together a freelance income while building their personal brands. Since one group pays the other — or doesn't, as the case may be — the two sides are engaged in a symbiotic dance around the issue of valuation. "I don't think anybody has any idea of what anyone should be paid for a piece anymore," Sicha says. "It's more than $25, but less than a thousand ... I think?" He added that, as of now, the Awl doesn't pay much to anyone, including himself.

The question of how journalists should be paid is of intense interest to journalists, obviously, but it matters to readers too, in ways they may not realize. Structures of compensation affect the end product, especially when salaries or bonuses are tied to the pursuit of traffic, a model that many online start-ups follow. Established publications — some of which are instituting or contemplating similar schemes — are watching the experiment with curiosity and trepidation. Writers and editors know that click-driven Internet economics tend to reward low-brow gimmickry. They have to decide whether to work around that or to embrace it as a fact of life.

One of the loudest proponents of the latter perspective is Henry Blodget, the editor in chief of Business Insider, a gossipy start-up. His talented staff breaks plenty of news and turns out the occasional high-prestige feature, but Blodget is unapologetic about mixing in a lot of eye candy and isn't above illustrating articles about A.I.G.'s woes with unrelated photos of attractive women kissing. A former star stock analyst who was banned from the profession amid accusations of securities fraud — he paid $4 million to settle — he says he sees himself as a journalistic outsider, unencumbered by the weight of conventional wisdom. In March he wrote: "Perhaps it's time to float a new theory: We're already in the gutter. What we click on accurately reflects what we're interested in, no matter how much we think and protest and hope to the contrary." A few days afterward, Blodget engaged in an entertaining multiplatform spat over the issue with the Reuters columnist Felix Salmon, producing the calculation that, in order to earn back a $60,000 annual salary, an online journalist needs to generate a whopping 1.8 million page views a month.

Blodget takes a lot of flak for his iconoclasm, but the fact is, he's only stating plainly what other editors think in private. If you don't believe that, check out the list of the most popular posts on your favorite Web site sometime — sex, scandal and Sarah Palin always score high. Even publications that don't go fishing for clicks discover that, inevitably, certain stories rise to the top. Charles Sennott told me that amid all of GlobalPost's serious coverage of wars and earthquakes, two big hits during the site's first year were a post titled, "Meet India's First Porn Star," and a slide show of Japanese cat outfits.

There is, of course, nothing wrong with giving readers what they secretly want every once in a while. The problem arises when you start producing articles solely for the id of the search engines, because some clicks are more valuable than others. This is the conclusion, at least, of Gawker Media's Nick Denton, one of the first to pay writers according to their page views and now a high-profile skeptic of the practice. Denton built his company on the labor of freelance bloggers, but in the last year, he has moved to hiring them as full-time employees, with set salaries and bonuses tied to "unique visitors" — a metric that he says measures the writer's ability to bring new readers into the fold. No sentimentalist, Denton says he changed the formula because he found that page-view incentives encouraged writers to deliver worthless rehashes rather than reporting and tabloid-style scoops — in other words, journalism.

"When we look at the numbers, it's increasingly evident that the traditional blog post has become a complete commodity," Denton says. When dueling algorithms compete to answer every human query, it turns out there's value in telling people things they weren't aware they didn't know. To wit: Denton's technology site Gizmodo recently bought a secret prototype iPhone that an Apple programmer lost in a bar and produced a post featuring pictures and the phone's specs. Over two weeks, that item racked up nearly 10 million page views, an estimated 4.4 million of them from newcomers, bringing the site an enormous amount of attention (not the least of it from Apple's lawyers and the police). Denton says his hope is that all the publicity attached to breaking big stories will translate into reader loyalty, brand equity and more lucrative advertising deals.

If that is the model of the future, then the new world could end up looking a lot like the old one, albeit with smaller newsrooms and new players. Politico replaces the Washington correspondent, TMZ is the gossip page and you can get coverage of your baseball team directly from MLB.com, which employs professional sportswriters. In cities like San Diego, New York and Washington, online start-ups are taking on metro news coverage, hoping to tap local ad markets. All of these publications have been hiring real, full-time employees — as have non-traditional providers like Yahoo, which is constructing a new political news site. Over the last few months, there has been a palpable uptick in both advertising and the journalism job market. The iPad, and its applications that restore magazines and newspapers to something like their traditional format, was greeted within the industry like the sight of a ship from a deserted island.

Still, it's hard to foresee anything like a total restoration. Many publications are struggling to stay afloat, from storied titles like Newsweek, which was recently put up for sale, to scrappy start-ups like The Faster Times. One April evening, Sam Apple and nine top staff members of the publication gathered at the foreign editor's place, a row house in Greenpoint, Brooklyn, to talk over their prospects. Apple presented what he believed to be the best route forward: introducing a membership program.

Readers could sign up to sponsor a favorite writer, at rates ranging from $12 to $120 a year. The writers would get 70 percent of the proceeds and in return would come up with customized benefits for their sponsors. Over beer and tortilla chips, the editors got to brainstorming. One contributor, a professor and translator of Nietzsche, had already offered to answer a philosophical question of the reader's choice. The dating columnist volunteered to critique online matchmaking profiles. Apple said that he'd just signed up a new writer. "She's a Sarah Lawrence grad, but also a dominatrix," he said. "She's going to be starting soon, writing about sex and power. So there's real incentive possibilities."

"Not to get too theoretical," the managing editor, Olivia Scheck, interjected over the laughter, "but this is the problem that we keep coming to with this idea, which is that we want to be selling journalism, not sex."

Apple mentioned, with some cheerful chagrin, that the site's most popular article ever in terms of page views was a blog post titled, "Megan Fox Has Wacky Hot Chick Syndrome." That wasn't exactly the kind of impact he had in mind when he came up with the idea for a new type of newspaper. But he said he liked to think that maybe a handful of those starlet-Googlers had stuck around to read the dispatches from Egypt and Turkey, or the acclaimed travel section, or the theater critic — who, contrary to all expectations, turned out to be The Faster Times's highest initial advertising earner.

Since I've been regularly reading The Faster Times, I've been most affected by a column called Financial Stress. Written by Kathryn Higgins, a single mother in Connecticut who is losing her house in foreclosure, it's a heartbreaking chronicle of unimaginable choices, like whether to squat or to move into a bedbug-infested homeless shelter. She just e-mailed Apple out of the blue one day, asking to contribute. There are a lot of voices like that in the Faster Times, writers who ended up on the wrong side of this recession. Whatever happens in the future, Apple has accomplished something by giving them a place to set their experiences down in words, creating a record of this transitional moment. That's the essence of journalism, but its value remains in the eye of the beholder.

ANDREW RICE is a contributing writer and the author of a book about Uganda, "The Teeth May Smile but the Heart Does Not Forget."

Bezos, Amazon's Founder, to Buy The Washington Post

BY CHRISTINE HAUGHNEY | AUG. 5, 2013

THE WASHINGTON POST, the newspaper whose reporting helped topple a president and inspired a generation of journalists, is being sold for $250 million to the founder of Amazon.com, Jeffrey P. Bezos, in a deal that has shocked the industry.

Donald E. Graham, chairman and chief executive of The Washington Post Company, and the third generation of the Graham family to lead the paper, told the staff about the sale late Monday afternoon. They had gathered together in the newspaper's auditorium at the behest of the publisher, Katharine Weymouth, his niece.

"I, along with Katharine Weymouth and our board of directors, decided to sell only after years of familiar newspaper-industry challenges made us wonder if there might be another owner who would be better for the Post (after a transaction that would be in the best interest of our shareholders)," Mr. Graham said in a written statement.

In the auditorium, he closed his remarks by saying that nobody in the room should be sad — except, he said, "for me."

The announcement was greeted by what many staff members described as "shock," a reaction shared in newsrooms across the country as one of the crown jewels of newspapers was surrendered by one of the industry's royal families.

In Mr. Bezos, The Post will have a very different owner, a technologist whose fortunes have risen in the last dozen years even as those of The Post and most newspapers have struggled. Through Amazon, the retailing giant, he has helped revolutionize the way people around the world consume — first books, then expanding to all kinds of goods and more recently in online storage, electronic books and online video, including a recent spate of original programming.

In the meeting, Mr. Graham stressed that Mr. Bezos would purchase The Post in a personal capacity and not on behalf of Amazon the company. The $250 million deal includes all of the publishing businesses owned by The Washington Post Company, including the Express newspaper, The Gazette Newspapers, Southern Maryland Newspapers, Fairfax County Times, El Tiempo Latino and Greater Washington Publishing.

The Washington Post company plans to hold on to Slate magazine, The Root.com and Foreign Policy. According to the release, Mr. Bezos has asked Ms. Weymouth to remain at The Post along with Stephen P. Hills, president and general manager; Martin Baron, executive editor; and Fred Hiatt, editor of the editorial page.

Mr. Bezos, who did not attend the meeting at The Post on Monday, said in a statement that he had known Mr. Graham for the past decade and said about Mr. Graham that "I do not know a finer man." Ms. Weymouth said that in negotiating this deal, Mr. Bezos made it clear he was not purely focused on profits.

The sale, at a price that would have been unthinkably low even a few years ago, represents the end of eight decades of ownership by the Graham family of The Post since Eugene Meyer bought The Post at auction on June 1, 1933. His son-in-law Philip L. Graham served as president of the paper from 1947 until his death in 1963. Then Graham's widow, Katharine Graham, oversaw the paper through the publication of the Pentagon Papers alongside The New York Times and its coverage of Watergate, the political scandal that led to the resignation of Richard Nixon and also a starring role for the newspaper in the film, "All The President's Men."

The Post's daily circulation peaked in 1993 at 832,332, according to the Alliance for Audited Media. But like most newspapers, it has suffered greatly from circulation and advertising declines. By March, the newspaper's daily circulation had dropped to 474,767.

The company became pressed enough for cash that Ms. Weymouth announced in February that it was looking to sell its flagship head-

CHRISTOPHER GREGORY/THE NEW YORK TIMES

The entrance of The Washington Post building on Monday.

quarters. According to a regulatory filing associated with the sale, Mr. Bezos will pay rent to The Post Company on the space for up to three years.

As of 2012, the newsroom, which once had more than 1,000 employees, had fewer than 640. People there on Monday described the mood as "somber" with "a lot of people kind of in disbelief."

In an interview in July, Mr. Graham was cagey about the family's future in the business. "I'll just fall back on the same answer," he said, adding, "In family companies you have judgments about the family and you have professional judgment. The family control of The Washington Post Company over the years, I think, has been a healthy thing."

In an e-mail Monday, Ms. Weymouth, who replaced her uncle as publisher in 2008, talked about the effect of the sale on her family: "Yes — we knew the sale was coming. This was a process that was months in the making. It is, of course, sad for the family — we have been incredibly honored to have been a part of The Post for the past

80, but we have always understood that this is a public trust and our focus was on ensuring that it would remain strong for generations of readers to come."

The Post is not the only newspaper to move to new ownership. The New York Times Company announced early Saturday morning that it had sold its New England Media Group, which includes The Boston Globe, for $70 million, a fraction of the $1.1 billion the Times company paid for just The Globe in 1993. Ken Doctor, an analyst at Outsell, said that the Post sale reflected a broader trend of newspaper ownership returning to local investors rather than large, publicly traded enterprises.

"Newspapers are not really much creatures of the marketplace anymore," said Mr. Doctor. "They're not throwing off much in profits. They need shelter from the pressure of quarterly financial statements and reports."

Newspaper analysts also said that the sale seems to be good news for the future of The Post. Alan D. Mutter, a newspaper consultant who writes the blog Reflections of a Newsosaur, said that for the first time someone with a native digital background was purchasing a major newspaper rather than an old-time businessman who would try to restore The Post to its earlier heyday and treat it "like 1953 Plymouths in Cuba."

While Mr. Bezos may be purchasing The Post separate from Amazon, Mr. Mutter predicted that there could be collaborations between the brands, like The Post's content appearing on every Kindle or Post video content appearing on Amazon.

"This is a guy who literally has invested in building rockets because he thinks it's a good idea. I believe he's bought the newspaper because he wants to re-envision the enterprise and The Post is an iconic world brand," said Mr. Mutter about Mr. Bezos. "He knows something about building iconic world brands."

Shortly after the announcement, Leonard Downie, the Post's former executive editor, sat down at the Caribou Coffee store down the

CHRISTOPHER GREGORY/THE NEW YORK TIMES

A Washington Post newspaper box in Washington on Monday.

block from the newsroom he once led and contemplated a future where the Grahams no longer own the newspaper.

Mr. Graham had called Mr. Downie, now a vice president at The Post Company, earlier in the day. "I was completely shocked," Mr. Downie said. "I could hardly say anything."

Mr. Downie arrived at the paper nearly 50 years ago, and for all of the time since, the Graham family has been at the center of the newspaper — and more broadly, he said, at the center of journalism in Washington.

"The important thing about the Grahams for me," he said, referring to Ben Bradlee, his predecessor as executive editor, "is that starting with Ben and with me, and I assume my successors, is that the news decisions were always ours, but the Grahams were always behind us."

MICHAEL D. SHEAR, **SHERYL GAY STOLBERG** and **SARAH WHEATON** contributed reporting.

How Facebook Is Changing the Way Its Users Consume Journalism

BY RAVI SOMAIYA | OCT. 26, 2014

MENLO PARK, CALIF. — Many of the people who read this article will do so because Greg Marra, 26, a Facebook engineer, calculated that it was the kind of thing they might enjoy.

Mr. Marra's team designs the code that drives Facebook's News Feed — the stream of updates, photographs, videos and stories that users see. He is also fast becoming one of the most influential people in the news business.

Facebook now has a fifth of the world — about 1.3 billion people — logging on at least monthly. It drives up to 20 percent of traffic to news sites, according to figures from the analytics company SimpleReach. On mobile devices, the fastest-growing source of readers, the percentage is even higher, SimpleReach says, and continues to increase.

The social media company is increasingly becoming to the news business what Amazon is to book publishing — a behemoth that provides access to hundreds of millions of consumers and wields enormous power. About 30 percent of adults in the United States get their news on Facebook, according to a study from the Pew Research Center. The fortunes of a news site, in short, can rise or fall depending on how it performs in Facebook's News Feed.

Though other services, like Twitter and Google News, can also exert a large influence, Facebook is at the forefront of a fundamental change in how people consume journalism. Most readers now come to it not through the print editions of newspapers and magazines or their home pages online, but through social media and search engines driven by an algorithm, a mathematical formula that predicts what users might want to read.

It is a world of fragments, filtered by code and delivered on demand. For news organizations, said Cory Haik, senior editor for digital news

SAM MANCHESTER/THE NEW YORK TIMES

at The Washington Post, the shift represents "the great unbundling" of journalism. Just as the music industry has moved largely from selling albums to songs bought instantly online, publishers are increasingly reaching readers through individual pieces rather than complete editions of newspapers or magazines. A publication's home page, said Edward Kim, a co-founder of SimpleReach, will soon be important more as an advertisement of its brand than as a destination for readers.

"People won't type in WashingtonPost.com anymore," Ms. Haik said. "It's search and social."

The shift raises questions about the ability of computers to curate news, a role traditionally played by editors. It also has broader implications for the way people consume information, and thus how they see the world.

In an interview at Facebook's sprawling headquarters here, which has a giant, self-driving golf cart that takes workers between buildings, Mr. Marra said he did not think too much about his impact on journalism.

"We try to explicitly view ourselves as not editors," he said. "We don't want to have editorial judgment over the content that's in your feed. You've made your friends, you've connected to the pages that you want to connect to and you're the best decider for the things that you care about."

In Facebook's work on its users' news feeds, Mr. Marra said, "we're saying, 'We think that of all the stuff you've connected yourself to, this is the stuff you'd be most interested in reading.' "

Roughly once a week, he and his team of about 16 adjust the complex computer code that decides what to show a user when he or she first logs on to Facebook. The code is based on "thousands and thousands" of metrics, Mr. Marra said, including what device a user is on, how many comments or likes a story has received and how long readers spend on an article.

The goal is to identify what users most enjoy, and its results vary around the world. In India, he said, people tend to share what the company calls the ABCDs: astrology, Bollywood, cricket and divinity.

JIM WILSON/THE NEW YORK TIMES

Facebook's Menlo Park, Calif., campus. A study says 30 percent of adults in America get news from the social network.

If Facebook's algorithm smiles on a publisher, the rewards, in terms of traffic, can be enormous. If Mr. Marra and his team decide that users do not enjoy certain things, such as teaser headlines that lure readers to click through to get all the information, it can mean ruin. When Facebook made changes to its algorithm in December 2013 to emphasize higher-quality content, several so-called viral sites that had thrived there, including Upworthy, Distractify and Elite Daily, saw large declines in their traffic.

Facebook executives frame the company's relationship with publishers as mutually beneficial: when publishers promote their content on Facebook, its users have more engaging material to read, and the publishers get increased traffic driven to their sites. Numerous publications, including The New York Times, have met with Facebook officials to discuss how to improve their referral traffic.

The increased traffic can potentially mean that the publisher can increase its advertising rates or convert some of those new readers into subscribers.

Social media companies like Facebook, Twitter and LinkedIn want their users to spend more time, or do more, on their services — a concept known as engagement, said Sean Munson, an assistant professor at the University of Washington who studies the intersection of technology and behavior.

Facebook officials say that the more time users spend at its site, the more likely there will be a robust exchange of diverse viewpoints and ideas shared online. Others fear that users will create their own echo chambers, and filter out coverage they do not agree with. "And that," Mr. Munson said, "is when you get conspiracy theories."

Ben Smith, editor in chief of BuzzFeed, a news and entertainment site, said his rule for writing and reporting in a fragmented age is simple: "no filler." News organizations that still publish a print edition, he said, have slots — physical holes on paper or virtual ones on a home page — that result in the publication of stories that are not necessarily the most interesting or timely, but are required to fill the space. It was partly to discourage such slot-filling that BuzzFeed did not focus on its home page when it first started, he said.

Mr. Kim of SimpleReach says he advises established media companies that "it's dangerous to start chasing social. You'll end up like everyone else, and you'll lose your differentiation." The question that older publications that are not "digital natives" like BuzzFeed have to ask themselves, Mr. Kim said, is "Are you creating content for the way that content is consumed in this environment?"

Ms. Haik, the Washington Post digital editor, is leading a team, started this year, that aims to deliver different versions of The Post's journalism to different people, based on information about how they have come to an article, which device they are on and even, if it is a phone, which way they are holding it.

"We're asking if there's a different kind of storytelling, not just an ideal presentation," she said. For instance, she said, people reading

The Post on a mobile phone during the day will probably want a different kind of reading experience than those who are on a Wi-Fi connection at home in the evening.

The Post is putting time and energy into such efforts, Ms. Haik said, because it is "ultimately about sustaining our business or growing our audience." More than half of its mobile readers, she said, are so-called millennials who consume news digitally and largely through social media sites like Facebook. Some publications have found a niche in taking the opposite approach. The Browser is edited by Robert Cottrell, a former journalist at The Financial Times and The Economist. Mr. Cottrell skims about 1,000 articles a day, he said, and then publishes five or six that he finds interesting for about 7,000 subscribers who pay $20 a year. A recent selection included the life of an early-20th-century American bricklayer and a study of great Eastern philosophers.

"The general idea is to offer a few pieces each day which we think are both enjoyable and of lasting value," Mr. Cottrell said. "We're certainly at the other end of the process from the algorithms."

Artificial intelligence, he said, may eventually be able to find a piece of writing moving, in some sense, and want to share it. But for the moment, computers rely on information gathered online "and that is going to be a very, very impoverished data set compared to a human being."

Mr. Marra, the Facebook engineer, agrees that a human editor for each individual would be ideal. "But it's not realistic to do that at scale for every person on the planet," he said, "and so I think we'll always have these hybrid systems like News Feed that are helping you find the things that you care about." It is simply, he said, "a personalized newspaper."

Why the Latest Layoffs Are Devastating to Democracy

OPINION | BY FARHAD MANJOO | JAN. 30, 2019

Digital media has always been a turbulent business, but last week's layoffs suggest a reason for panic.

WORKING IN DIGITAL MEDIA is like trying to build a fort out of marshmallows on a foundation made of marbles in a country ruled by capricious and tyrannical warring robots. I've toiled in this business for nearly 20 years, and even in the best of times it has been a squeamish and skittering ride, the sort of career you'd counsel your kids to avoid in favor of something less volatile and more enduring — bitcoin mining, perhaps.

It might be tempting, then, to dismiss the recent spate of media-biz layoffs as unfortunate but otherwise not concerning. Two hundred workers, including dozens of journalists, were given the slip last week at BuzzFeed. About 800 people are losing their jobs in the media division of Verizon, the telephone company that owns Yahoo, HuffPost, TechCrunch and many other "content brands." And Gannett, the once-mighty newspaper empire that owns USA Today and hundreds of smaller outlets — from The Bergen County Record to The Zanesville Times Recorder — is letting go of 400.

But it would be a mistake to regard these cuts as the ordinary chop of a long-roiling digital media sea. Instead, they are a devastation.

The cause of each company's troubles may be distinct, but collectively the blood bath points to the same underlying market pathology: the inability of the digital advertising business to make much meaningful room for anyone but monopolistic tech giants.

Coming in a time of economic prosperity, at world-historical levels of interest in the news, last week's cuts tell a story of impending slow-motion doom — and a democratic emergency in the making, with no end in sight.

Consider: We are in the midst of a persistent global information war. We live our lives on technologies that sow distrust and fakery, that admit little room for nuance and complication, that slice us up into ignorant and bleating tribes. It is an era that should be ripe for journalists and for the business of journalism — a profession that, though it errs often, is the best way we know of inoculating ourselves against the suffocating deluge of rumor and mendacity.

And for a while, it looked like we could do that. The past half decade has been a season of bold and optimistic innovation in media. In addition to the Trump bump, there was new money from venture capitalists, and giants in cable and telecom. Big brands, looking to attract millennials, began to spend haltingly and then generously on advertising, leading to a Cambrian explosion of new sites, new formats, new business models. And consumers began opening up their wallets to support journalism, turning around the fortunes of The New York Times.

Many in the industry remain optimistic about these ways forward. There's a doubling-down on subscriptions, a rush to podcasts and high-end video, and a return to smaller and more calculated media ventures, like Bill Simmons's tiny but profitable start-up, The Ringer. Then there is the charity of digital billionaires. The Craig Newmark Graduate School of Journalism, Jeff Bezos' Washington Post, Laurene Powell Jobs's Atlantic magazine, Marc Benioff's Time and Farhad Manjoo's Color Me Skeptical That the Billionaires Who Got Us Into This Mess Will Save Us Gazette.

But it takes only a quick jaunt through the particulars of last week's layoffs to snuff out much reason for optimism.

In the cuts at Gannett, we see the nearly final evisceration of local news, an institution recognized as democratically vital even by the mainstream media's most frothing detractors. Gannett's end now looks nigh; the company is presently laboring under a hostile takeover bid by a secretive hedge fund whose only demonstrated expertise lies in "strip-mining" publications of their final morsels of profit.

In the troubles at Verizon, we see a behemoth that tried to take on Google and Facebook. Under a former executive, Tim Armstrong, the phone company bought up Yahoo and other media brands as useful pawns in a strategic war against internet giants. For similar reasons, Comcast has also plowed money into media start-ups.

But Verizon quickly learned that Facebook and Google are insurmountable. When new management took over last year, it began dumping the news in favor of readier ways to make money.

It's the cuts at BuzzFeed that sting most. You may regard the site as a purveyor of silly listicles and inane quizzes. I think of it as a relentlessly experimental innovator: It's the site that gave us The Dress and published The Dossier, a company that pushed the rest of the industry to regard the digital world with seriousness and rigor.

More than anyone else in media, BuzzFeed's founder, Jonah Peretti, bet on symbioses with the tech platforms. He understood that the tech giants would keep getting bigger, but to him that was a feature, not a bug. By creating content that hooked into their algorithms, he imagined BuzzFeed getting bigger — and making money — along with them.

At the least, the layoffs suggest the tragic folly of Mr. Peretti's thinking. Google and Facebook have no economic incentive for symbiosis; everything BuzzFeed can do for them can also be done by the online hordes who'll make content without pay.

So where does that leave media? Bereft.

It is the rare publication that can survive on subscriptions, and the rarer one that will be saved by billionaires. Digital media needs a way to profitably serve the masses. If even BuzzFeed couldn't hack that, we are well and truly hosed.

FARHAD MANJOO became an opinion columnist for The Times in 2018. Before that, he wrote the State of the Art column. He is the author of "True Enough: Learning to Live in a Post-Fact Society."

Digital Media: What Went Wrong

BY EDMUND LEE | FEB. 1, 2019

For years, BuzzFeed seemed to be leading the journalism industry toward a brave new future. Now that it has stumbled, the way ahead looks more old-school than ever.

THE DIGITAL PUBLISHING INDUSTRY took a big hit in recent days, when more than 1,000 employees were laid off at BuzzFeed, AOL, Yahoo and HuffPost. Vice Media started the process of laying off some 250 workers on Friday, and Mic, a site aimed at younger readers, axed much of its staff two months ago before a competitor bought it in a fire sale. Coupled with recent layoffs at Gannett, the company behind USA Today and other dailies nationwide, the crisis in the digital sphere suggested that the journalism business was damned if it embraced innovation and damned if it didn't.

The cuts at BuzzFeed were the most alarming. Wasn't this the company that was supposed to have it all figured out? Didn't its team of wizards, led by the M.I.T.-trained chief executive, Jonah Peretti, know tricks of the digital trade that lay beyond the imagination of fusty old print publishers?

Chris Hayes, the author and MSNBC anchor, summed up the bleak outlook with a tweet that asked, "What if there is literally no profitable model for digital news?"

The in-the-moment doomsaying was understandable. But look past the gloom, and a complicated narrative emerges that does not lend itself to a one-size-fits-all interpretation of What Went Wrong or a handy forecast of journalism's future.

While leading digital publishers have resorted to harsh measures, legacy titles such as The Washington Post, The Atlantic, The New Yorker and The New York Times have seen growth as they accommodate the habits of their increasingly digitally oriented readers.

At the same time, a digital-native business, Vox Media, the owner of The Verge and Eater, turned a profit last year, its first as a large company, according to two people with knowledge of the matter who were not authorized to discuss it publicly. And a more recent digital upstart, Axios, a buzzy site for Beltway insiders created by the founders of Politico, expects a profit in 2019, according to its chief executive, Jim VandeHei.

Even BuzzFeed may hit its financial marks this year. If it does, the reason will most likely be a combination of old-school business methods tried elsewhere (including layoffs), rather than its ability to crack some esoteric digital code.

GOING AROUND FACEBOOK

It was simpler in the days of print. Even when radio and television laid waste to certain newspapers and magazines, the industry as a whole racked up steady profits. Twentieth-century readers were more or less unchanging in their habits, so media executives did not have to revise their business models much from year to year.

That has changed, to say the least.

Mr. Peretti seemed to be on the right track with his reliance on sponsored posts to generate revenue before his reluctant pivot to banner ads last year. That money encouraged him to stick to his idea of creating free content that readers can't resist sharing on social media. Hedging his bets, he varied BuzzFeed's money stream by selling branded cookware in association with Wal-Mart and opening a toy store in Manhattan.

The company's revenue grew more than 15 percent in 2018 — not quite enough to stave off Mr. Peretti's decision to cut about 220 of BuzzFeed's roughly 1,500 employees. As he put it in a recent staff memo, "Unfortunately, revenue growth by itself isn't enough to be successful in the long run."

Ben Thompson, an analyst who has become a favorite among the Silicon Valley set, argued that BuzzFeed had inadvertently devalued its content by mostly relying on the kindness of digital giants to distribute its articles.

Facebook's changes to its News Feed in recent years increased the visibility of posts from your aunts and uncles while playing down articles from professional publishers. That was no good for sites like BuzzFeed.

"The only way to build a thriving business in a space dominated by an aggregator is to go around them, not to work with them," Mr. Thompson wrote in his Jan. 28 newsletter.

DIGITAL REVOLUTION? MORE LIKE EVOLUTION

In BuzzFeed's youth, Facebook was not the dominant traffic driver it is today, and online sharing was just as likely to occur away from social media platforms. (Remember email?) Five years into its existence, in 2011, the site got newsier, with the addition of Politico's Ben Smith as its editor in chief, along with a team of editors and reporters. In 2015, Mr. Thompson, the analyst, called BuzzFeed "the most important news organization in the world."

After that, Mr. Peretti adjusted his approach again. He determined that Facebook had already built the pipes for distribution, so instead of trying to amass audiences around a single venue, like BuzzFeed.com, he went where the audience was: Facebook.

That was back when Facebook was considered a natural ally for media organizations seeking millions of online readers, and before Mark Zuckerberg, its chief executive, was made to testify before skeptical lawmakers in Washington and Brussels.

So publishers didn't balk when Facebook asked them — as part of its plan to take on YouTube — to go big on video. Companies like BuzzFeed, Vox Media and Refinery29 had an additional incentive to go along with Facebook's request: the ad dollars that had shifted online as viewers started to favor streaming services over traditional television.

The plan proved difficult to monetize, however. Facebook wanted brevity, but it defied common sense to load a 15-second commercial in front of a 30-second clip, Mr. Peretti said in a November interview with The Times.

In 2017, Facebook created a new section, Facebook Watch, that featured longer videos. The company also opened more of those videos to advertising last August. For publishers, it was an improvement, but still not enough.

"They need to make a lot more progress to truly compensate for the value that media companies are creating for them," Mr. Peretti said in the interview. He compared Facebook to cable operators like Comcast, which pay programmers to carry their shows. "Except the compensation isn't like cable," he added.

As television viewers continued their migration to the web, big TV companies like NBCUniversal, Turner Broadcasting and Discovery Communications followed them, plowing hundreds of millions of dollars into digital companies.

Now they would like to see a return on their investments. And they are getting impatient.

OLD-SCHOOL DIGITAL

It wasn't supposed to be this hard for digital publishers.

In 2011, when The Times drew criticism for its decision to charge online readers, creating a so-called paywall, BuzzFeed was taking off, thanks to its knack for harnessing the power of social networks. In that context, the paywall strategy struck media gurus as the last-ditch gambit of a slow-moving stalwart, and the conventional wisdom was that digital mastersmiths would soon outperform or perhaps even vanquish their print-beholden rivals.

By the end of 2018, the picture looked vastly different. BuzzFeed generated more than $300 million in sales, while still bleeding money, and The Times was on a pace to exceed $650 million in digital revenue.

A stormy sociopolitical climate played to the strengths of seasoned media companies. John Wagner, who handles ad spending for publisher properties for the media agency PHD, said that during the

Trump presidency, advertisers had favored venerable publications like The Times, The Washington Post and The Wall Street Journal. News sites of 21st-century vintage, on the other hand, have to keep proving themselves.

"BuzzFeed has really good offerings," Mr. Wagner said. But its listicles and quizzes, he added, may eventually fall out of favor. "Consumers are fickle, and they'll move on to the next thing," he said.

Mr. VandeHei of Axios said media companies needed more than digital savvy to make it in the current cutthroat environment. "I think media is still a great business, if you run it like a damn business," he said in an email.

Mr. VandeHei recited a litany of plagues on the digital houses, such as taking investments from venture capitalists expecting big returns in a short time or tying audience growth to platforms like Facebook.

With its reliance on sponsored newsletters, Axios has a business model wildly different from BuzzFeed's. ("I'm an outlier," Mr. VandeHei said.) But while a comparison of the two companies may not be apples to apples, the debate over journalism's future comes down to which business model works better — or works at all.

Axios generated more than $24 million in revenue last year while incurring an overall loss of $56,000, Mr. VandeHei said. He credited a simple reason for its success: "The audience for high-quality content is huge and voracious and growing." And the company's focus on newsletters means it is unaffected by the whims of Facebook.

The Information, a San Francisco tech-news site founded in 2013, is another digital publisher that adopted an old-fashioned business model from the start: paid subscriptions.

"Journalism has been paid for since its early days," Jessica Lessin, the founder and chief executive of The Information, said in an interview. From her perspective, the tendency of news media executives to give their content away once they moved to the web was the result of something like amnesia.

"We just forgot," she said. "We all went online and threw that out."

Ms. Lessin, a former reporter for The Wall Street Journal, declined to disclose the exact number of readers who pay $399 annually, but said the publication had "tens of thousands of subscribers." While that audience is relatively modest, it allowed her to double her staff last year to 26 journalists.

"Subscription is a great business," Ms. Lessin said. "We are covering and expanding at the pace we want to expand off subscription, since that revenue can be very predictable."

While BuzzFeed and HuffPost have remained anti-paywall, and Axios and The Information have depended on sponsorships or subscriptions, Vox Media has found a middle way.

Jim Bankoff, the company's chief executive, is more business oriented than his peers and rarely calls attention to himself. A former AOL executive, he has explored areas outside of traditional advertising as part of his approach.

One result was a production agreement with Netflix for a series based on Vox's explanatory journalism, "Explained." The company has also generated revenue by building its conference business, getting into podcasting and licensing its content management system, Chorus.

Last year, its revenue increased 20 percent to around $185 million, for a modest profit. But that doesn't mean Vox has stumbled onto some wild innovation.

"We don't see ourselves as a digital media company," Mr. Bankoff said. "I mean, is anybody only just that now? We're a modern media company."

JACLYN PEISER contributed reporting.

EDMUND LEE covers the media industry as it grapples with changes from Silicon Valley. Before joining The Times he was the managing editor at Vox Media's Recode.

CHAPTER 5

Spotlight on Journalists

While this volume has thus far considered the history of journalism and The New York Times, this chapter offers an opportunity to learn about the lives and contributions of particular journalists. These articles also cover the potential dangers of reporting, and how the commitment to a story has made some American journalists the targets of threats and violence.

Fighting for Press Freedom in a Dangerous World

BY JOYCE WADLER | FEB. 27, 2002

WHAT'S THIS E-MAIL MESSAGE that's popped up at the office of the Committee to Protect Journalists? Something about a luncheon in Washington featuring a dermatologist known as the Botox Queen at which the organizers want to announce a benefit for Daniel Pearl?

It strikes Ann K. Cooper, the executive director of the Committee to Protect Journalists, as kind of funny: it's unexpected to see a mention of the Botox Queen, although the offer is appreciated and will be accepted.

As for how it was last Thursday when her organization, which works for press freedom worldwide, learned about the murder of Mr. Pearl, the Wall Street Journal reporter who was abducted in Pakistan last month and later killed by his captors, it was, as one would expect, a terrible day. All at once, all the phones were screaming.

Was Ms. Cooper able to sleep the night she learned of Mr. Pearl's death?

"I slept that night because I took a sleeping pill," she says. "I knew it was going to be hard."

She has a National Public Radio way of talking: intelligent, informed, no discernible accent, which makes sense, for she was for several years an NPR reporter, working, for a spell, from Moscow. Learning the business of journalism, she was the sort of reporter who found the hearings on the desalination plant in her hometown, Yuma, Ariz., fascinating. When she displays a Lenin paperweight with an inspirational slogan in Russian (strictly for entertainment value), it is not a surprise to hear the words, "I'll have to transliterate this."

Her memory, on international events, is excellent. The scariest time in her life as a foreign correspondent: January 1991, in Lithuania, when the Russians decided to crack down, and the tanks rolled in. The turret of a tank spun around so that she and the tank were sort of eye to eye.

The year she met her husband, Larry Heinzerling, an editor at The Associated Press, takes longer to recall, although she beams when you zoom in on her wedding picture, taken last year. The bride wore red.

"The best day of my life," Ms. Cooper says.

She is not without a sense of fun. In her office, among the many photos of her husband and 12-year-old son, she has three sets of Russian nesting dolls, including the Beatles. Who are those grim fellows near the Fab Four?

"They were the leaders of a coup d'état against Gorbachev in 1991," Ms. Cooper says. "I found them in a flea market and thought, These I must have. Considering the circumstance, I would think they're very rare."

The Committee to Protect Journalists publicizes, and in that way pressures, governments or groups that have harassed, imprisoned or murdered reporters. According to its research, 37 journalists were killed last year, 118 were imprisoned. With a budget of $2.5 million, the group cannot to pay the legal bills for everyone, but it does expedite things. The committee puts reporters in touch with groups that can provide funds, and it provides some legal help and money.

The daughter of a hardware store manager and an elementary school teacher, Ms. Cooper, 52, graduated from Iowa State University and covered Washington for The Capitol Hill News Service and Congressional Quarterly.

When her husband at the time, Bill Keller, was sent to Russia in 1986 as a correspondent for The New York Times, she became a correspondent for NPR, later covering South Africa and the United Nations. Ms. Cooper and Mr. Keller later divorced. Ms. Cooper joined the Committee to Protect Journalists in 1998.

A case that makes her feel good?

The story of Abner Machuca, a sound man for Chilean state TV who was shot in the head by a sniper at the Kosovo-Albania border in 1999. It is not difficult to put a face on Mr. Machuca: there is a color photo of him at the committee's office, a solid, dark-haired man, being carried by his arms and legs by terrified colleagues. Mr. Machuca's face has the blank look of someone who has been knocked out, although his eyes are open.

"Our thought was, What can we do here in New York?" Ms. Cooper says. "Abner's editors in Chile just wanted to be able to get through to the hospital in Albania where he was taken, so we got a hookup through a CNN satellite phone. They wanted to medevac him out as soon as possible, which was nighttime, and NATO controlled the skies and was not allowing flights in and out. I drafted a letter to NATO and called someone I knew from NPR and she walked it in and they gave us clearance. He made a full recovery."

Another success story, please, for the murder of a journalist hangs heavy.

Ms. Cooper offers up the case of Aroun Rashid Deen, a Sierra Leone television reporter, along with some of his footage. It shows victims of the Revolutionary United Front whose arms or legs had been hacked off. When those reports were used as trial evidence,

Mr. Deen's life was threatened. The committee gave him a ticket to the United States.

He's in the office a lot now, Ms. Cooper says. He was a sports reporter in Sierra Leone, but it's unlikely he'll be able to get that sort of work here. He's doing temp work and working in a nursing home.

Death by Terror

EDITORIAL | BY THE NEW YORK TIMES | AUG. 21, 2014

THE REACTION TO the terrible death of James Foley, the freelance journalist kidnapped and executed by Islamist extremists, comes in stages. First and foremost is the grief at the cruel death of a brave reporter who knowingly risked his life to tell a critical story.

Then comes horror at the sadism of the executioner, whose accent spoke of years spent in London. Could he be one of the many young foreigners who have joined the ranks of the Islamic State in Iraq and Syria, attracted by the perverse romance of "holy war?"

Finally there's the chilling knowledge that this is neither the first nor the last time we must witness the horror of a hostage kneeling before masked executioners. Seizing hostages for revenge, to terrorize, to make a political statement or to exact ransom has become a standard weapon in the arsenal of terrorists, leaving no journalist, humanitarian worker or traveler in a conflict zone immune.

All these motives appear to have figured in the fate of Mr. Foley. He was captured in Syria in November 2012, and before he was killed ISIS reportedly demanded 100 million euros ($132 million) in ransom, following Al Qaeda's practice in recent years of raising funds by abducting foreigners. But no money was paid for Mr. Foley, and a special operation failed to find him.

After the United States began airstrikes against ISIS forces in Iraq earlier this month, the group shifted to the infamous practices of Abu Musab al-Zarqawi, the leader of Al Qaeda in Iraq, who was known as "Sheikh of the Slaughterers" for the many foreign captives he decapitated. The masked man with the British accent who killed Mr. Foley said he was doing it in retaliation for the American airstrikes; at the end of the video that was released, he is shown holding another captive American freelance journalist, Steven Sotloff, as he says, "The life of this American citizen, Obama, depends on your next decision."

ARIS MESSINIS/AFP/GETTY IMAGES

U.S. freelance reporter James Foley resting in a room at the airport of Sirte, Libya on Sept. 29, 2011.

There will be those who argue that the United States is somehow responsible for Mr. Foley's death, either by refusing to pay a ransom or by bombing ISIS. But the history of political kidnapping suggests this is too simple. Kidnappings have been a staple of guerrilla warfare since they were popularized by Latin American revolutionaries in the 1970s, as has been the debate over whether to pay ransom. The United Nations estimated that about $30 million was paid out in ransom for political kidnappings in Latin America in 1973 alone.

The practice was exported around the world and especially to the Middle East, where many hostages, including journalists, were seized over the past decades. More recently, ransom income has played a major role in financing the Qaeda network — a recent report by Rukmini Callimachi in The Times found that more than 50 hostages have been seized by Al Qaeda over the past five years, and many have been ransomed for substantial sums paid by European governments.

Still, there have been changes in recent years. First is the cruelty of kidnapping foreigners purely to post their executions online. The beheading of Daniel Pearl, a Wall Street Journal reporter, by a top Qaeda operative in 2002 revealed the viciousness of the Islamic fanatics, a cruelty raised to new levels by ISIS. Second, while journalists are by no means the only victims — many more humanitarian and government workers have been seized — the death of Mr. Foley and the threat to Mr. Sotloff point to the special danger faced by the freelance reporters who have become more numerous in war zones with the proliferation of Internet news sites. Without the resources, credentials or experience of established news organizations, freelancers are often at greater risk in conflict zones.

There is no simple answer on whether to submit to terrorist extortion. The United States and Britain refuse to pay ransoms, and there is evidence that hostage takers target victims based on the potential for a payout. If everyone refused to pay, terrorists might not have had the incentive to turn kidnapping into an industry. At a Group of 8 summit meeting last year, Western countries agreed not to make ransom payments, but some European governments continue the practice.

In the meantime, we can honor the many brave journalists, aid workers and civil servants who risk their lives in conflict zones, and grieve for Mr. Foley and the many others who have lost their freedom or their lives.

Steven Sotloff, Journalist Held by ISIS, Was Undeterred by Risks of Job

BY RICK GLADSTONE AND SHREEYA SINHA | AUG. 22, 2014

STEVEN J. SOTLOFF, a 31-year-old freelance journalist, self-described "stand-up philosopher from Miami," immersed himself in the tumult of the Middle East for years, repeatedly venturing into some of the most hazardous conflict zones. He reassured friends that he knew the risks as he wrote for publications that included Time magazine, The Christian Science Monitor and World Affairs Journal.

The risks caught up with him a year ago when he was abducted in northern Syria as he reported on the civil war that is still convulsing that country, the most dangerous place for journalists, with more than 70 killed and 80 kidnapped since the conflict began.

A virtual news blackout on his fate was lifted on Tuesday when he appeared in an Internet video produced by the Islamic State in Iraq and Syria, the extremist group holding him hostage, that showed the beheading of James Foley, a 40-year-old fellow freelancer and abduction victim. The video showed a black-clad masked militant towering above Mr. Sotloff as he knelt in an orange jumpsuit, head shaved, with his captors warning that Mr. Sotloff would be the next to die as retribution for American airstrikes on ISIS targets in Iraq. The video ends with the militant warning President Obama, in English, that Mr. Sotloff's fate "depends on your next decision."

As of Friday, there was still no word on whether Mr. Sotloff had been killed.

Mr. Sotloff's family had desperately sought to keep his abduction quiet, apparently fearing publicity could further endanger him. But the strategy was upended when the world learned that Mr. Sotloff was an ISIS hostage. Although his family still urged Mr. Sotloff's friends not to talk, more than 8,100 people have signed a petition on the White House website, created on the same day the ISIS video was posted, urging Mr. Obama "to take immediate action to save Steven's life by any means necessary."

Described by friends as selfless, Mr. Sotloff spent most of his life in Florida except when he attended a boarding high school, Kimball Union Academy in Meriden, N.H., where he apparently developed a penchant for reporting and writing. He coedited the student newspaper, The Kimball Union, graduated in 2002 and attended the University of Central Florida, where he played rugby, worked for the independent student newspaper, Central Florida Future, and expressed deep interest in travel to the Middle East.

He left after three years and, soon after, began to pursue journalism full-time.

"The guy lit up a room. He was always such a loyal, caring and good friend to us," Josh Polsky, who shared a dormitory suite with Mr. Sotloff, said in a telephone interview. "If you needed to rely on anybody for anything he would drop everything on a dime for you or for anyone else."

Emerson Lotzia Jr., another former college roommate, said that Mr. Sotloff was undeterred by the risks of Middle East reporting. "A million people could have told him what he was doing was foolish, it seemed like it to us outsiders looking in, but to him it was what he loved to do and you weren't going to stop him," Mr. Lotzia told Central Florida Future on Wednesday. "Steve said it was scary over there. It was dangerous. It wasn't safe to be over there. He knew it. He kept going back."

An avid user of social media until his last posting on Aug. 3 of last year, when he ruminated about the Miami Heat basketball team, Mr. Sotloff described himself in his Twitter biography as a "Stand-up philosopher from Miami."

He wrote dispatches from conflicts in Bahrain, Egypt, Turkey, Libya and Syria. In one piece for Time about lawlessness in Libya, published in the aftermath of the deadly Sept. 11, 2012, attack on the American diplomatic compound in Benghazi that became a crisis for the

Obama administration, Mr. Sotloff was prophetic: "With no security organizations to ensure order and an ineffective justice system unable to prosecute suspects, Libyans fear their country is slowly crumbling around them."

In a report for World Affairs Journal last year from Egypt after the military coup that deposed Mohamed Morsi, the Muslim Brotherhood leader who was the country's first democratically elected president, Mr. Sotloff gave voice to Muslim Brotherhood supporters who felt disenfranchised. " 'The people voted for Morsi,' 45-year-old teacher Sa'id Rashwan told me. 'Why have a few now decided he cannot rule?' "

Anne Marlowe, a writer, said on her Twitter account that Mr. Sotloff had lived in Yemen for years, "spoke good Arabic, deeply loved Islamic world.... for this he is threatened with beheading."

Mr. Polsky, a lawyer, said that Mr. Sotloff's circle of college acquaintances, upon learning what had befallen their friend, immediately began contacting one another after having drifted apart over the years.

"This event has brought all of us back together," he said. "As soon as we learned of the circumstances, we all became in touch with one another again out of concern for Steve's well-being and to reminisce about our experiences of our collegial lives."

When Reporting Is Dangerous

OPINION | BY NICHOLAS KRISTOF | SEPT. 3, 2014

MY HEART BROKE for Steven Sotloff, the second American journalist beheaded in Syria, not only because of the barbarity ISIS inflicted on him but also because he died trying to push back against the trend in news coverage.

Over the last couple of decades, we've all seen trivialization of news, a drift toward celebrity, scandal and salaciousness.

So far this year, nightly newscasts on ABC, CBS and NBC have offered a combined total of 3 minutes of coverage of the civil war and impending famine in South Sudan, and 9 minutes about mass atrocities in Central African Republic, according to Andrew Tyndall of the Tyndall Report, which tracks such things. In contrast, the missing Malaysian airliner drew 304 minutes (almost five times as much as the Syrian civil war).

That's why this is a moment to honor Sotloff — and James Foley, the other American journalist executed, and so many others out on the front lines — not just for his physical courage, but also for his moral courage in trying to focus attention on neglected stories. He shone a spotlight in dark nooks of the world to help shape the global agenda.

It was a struggle for him.

"I've been here over a week and no one wants freelance because of the kidnappings," Sotloff emailed another journalist while in Syria before his kidnapping, according to Reuters. "It's pretty bad here. I've been sleeping at a front, hiding from tanks the past few nights, drinking rainwater."

One of the biggest changes that I've seen in my career is that journalists and aid workers have become targets. Virulent extremist groups now see journalists as enemies, and subject captives to abuse and torture. For instance, the Islamic State in Iraq and Syria reportedly waterboarded Foley before murdering him.

In addition, in conflict areas, any petty criminal with a gun can kidnap a journalist or aid worker and sell him or her to a group that will demand a ransom. European nations pay these ransoms, which both enrich the terror groups and create an incentive to kidnap other foreigners.

A Times investigation found that Al Qaeda and its direct affiliates had raised at least $125 million from kidnappings since 2008. That's a powerful business model for a terror group, and it's one reason journalism and aid work is more dangerous today.

Last year, 70 journalists were killed for doing their jobs, according to the Committee to Protect Journalists. Over the last few years, some 70 journalists have been killed while covering the Syrian conflict, and about 20 are missing.

Most of those are Syrian, and let's remember that the greatest danger is faced not by the Western journalists but by local ones — or by the local translators and drivers working for Western journalists.

In Darfur once, my interpreter and I were frantically interviewing villagers as a warlord was approaching to massacre them. Finally, my interpreter said: *We've just got to go. If they catch us, they'll hold you for ransom. But they'll just shoot me.*

We fled.

One way to honor Foley and Sotloff (and Daniel Pearl and many others killed over the years) would be for the United States to speak up more forcefully for journalists imprisoned by foreign governments — often by our friends, like Turkey or Ethiopia. Think of Eskinder Nega, serving an 18-year sentence in Ethiopia, or Somyot Prueksakasemsuk, a Thai serving 11 years for publishing articles deemed insulting to the king of Thailand.

Today there are Steven Sotloffs covering war in Ukraine, Ebola in Liberia, malnutrition in India — and also covering unemployment and crime in American cities.

They are indefatigable and relentless. Once while I was covering the Congo civil war with a group of Africa-based reporters, our plane crashed. It was terrifying for me, but another passenger (a reporter based in Nairobi) told me it was her third plane crash. Yet another colleague on that plane was later killed covering a conflict in West Africa.

A special shout-out to the photojournalists and video journalists, for they often take the greatest risks. A reporter like myself can keep a distance, while that's useless for those with cameras. My first rule of covering conflicts is never to accept a ride from photographers, because when they hear gunfire they rush toward it. Just Wednesday, it was confirmed that a Russian photojournalist, Andrei Stenin, had been killed in Ukraine.

So, to Steven Sotloff and James Foley and all brave journalists putting themselves in harm's way, whatever nationality, this column is a tribute to you — and to your loved ones, who suffer as well.

We mourn you; we miss you; and, we admire you. And your commitment to the serious over the salacious elevates not only journalism but the entire global society.

David Carr's Last Word on Journalism, Aimed at Students

WITH DAVID CARR | FEB. 15, 2015

DAVID CARR WAS KNOWN at The New York Times as a supreme talent scout, a mentor to young reporters and a blunt critic of those who didn't measure up. He was a natural teacher, and right up until the day he died last week, he was bent on minting the next generation of journalists. Last fall, David joined the faculty at Boston University's communications school. While David did not write his curriculum as a column, it has all the essential ingredients of one. So here it serves as the final Media Equation under David's byline.

"I love the current future of journalism we are living through and care desperately about getting my students ready to prosper in this new place," read the quotation below David's portrait in a photo gallery at B.U., where David served as the first Andrew R. Lack professor.

The class he taught offered a window into the future he was trying to shape. His course, called Press Play, focused on the cutting edge of media and was about "making and distributing content in the present future we are living through." David cared deeply about nurturing reporters-to-be — college students who felt the calling and were looking for a spiritual guide to help them navigate the rapidly shifting media landscape.

The syllabus for Press Play, published on the blogging platform Medium, is perhaps David's most succinct prescription for how to thrive in the digital age. It is also David in his purest form — at once blunt, funny, haughty, humble, demanding, endearing and unique.

David was interested in people, not their résumés. He didn't care where someone went to college or who their parents were. So instead of giving his students a standard biographical blurb (graduate of the University of Minnesota, editor of The Washington City Paper, media

RYAN PFLUGER FOR THE NEW YORK TIMES

David Carr at home in 2008.

columnist at The Times since 2005), David told them this, under the heading "Not need to know, but nice to know":

"Your professor is a terrible singer and a decent dancer. He is a movie crier but stone-faced in real life. He never laughs even when he is actually amused. He hates suck-ups, people who treat waitresses and cab drivers poorly and anybody who thinks diversity is just an academic conceit. He is a big sucker for the hard worker and is rarely dazzled by brilliance. He has little patience for people who pretend to ask questions when all they really want to do is make a speech.

"He has a lot of ideas about a lot of things, some of which are good. We will figure out which is which together. He likes being challenged. He is an idiosyncratic speaker, often beginning in the middle of a story, and is used to being told that people have no idea what he is talking about. It's fine to be one of those people. In Press Play, he will strive to be a lucid, linear communicator.

"Your professor is fair, fundamentally friendly, a little odd, but not very mysterious. If you want to know where you stand, just ask."

He encouraged teamwork. "While writing, shooting, and editing are often solitary activities, great work emerges in the spaces between people," David wrote, adding, "Evaluations will be based not just on your efforts, but on your ability to bring excellence out of the people around you."

David warned there would be a heavy reading list. "I'm not sliming you with a bunch of textbooks, so please know I am dead serious about these readings," he wrote. "Skip or skim at your peril."

Each of his classes and reading assignments spoke to specific pieces of his vision for the future. "You Are What You Type on" was the title of his Week 3 lecture, "a discussion of how, more and more, the medium is becoming the message." In Week 5, "New Business Models for Storytelling," David required the students to read "GE Becomes Legitimate Online News Publisher," a Digiday article that explored how General Electric was producing its own high-quality news content, known as "native advertising." A few weeks later, in a class called "Storytelling Innovations," David, a music nut, assigned Arcade Fire's "Reflektor," a trailblazing interactive video that the rock band produced along with Google.

As forward-thinking as David was, he also revered great journalism in the traditional sense. Sprinkled throughout the course list are pieces that have nothing to do with content management systems or multimedia packaging. He asked his students to read, before the semester began, Ta-Nehisi Coates's "The Case for Reparations," the provocative essay published last year in The Atlantic describing how blacks should be financially compensated for having been handicapped throughout American history. For the second week, he assigned "Consider the Lobster," David Foster Wallace's dispatch from the Maine Lobster Festival that considered whether it was "all right to boil a sentient creature alive just for our gustatory pleasure."

And as an exceptional writer with a unique voice, David did not forsake the opportunity to share those gifts. In a class called "Voice Lessons," he sought to teach students "how to quit sounding like everyone else and begin sounding like ... yourself."

"From asking me about my personal experiences and things that had happened in my life, he would give me advice specifically geared to me," said Prim Chuwiruch, 24, who is originally from Thailand and was a graduate student in David's first class. "He would say, 'These are things that you have that no one else does, and you should channel that.' "

In the curriculum, David said: "Who you are and what you have been through should give you a prism on life that belongs to you only. We will talk about the uses and abuses of a writer's voice, how to express yourself in copy without using the 'I' word and why ending stories with a quote from someone else is often the coward's way out."

Mikaela Lefrak, 26, was his teaching assistant his first semester. "He didn't want us to sound like everyone else," she wrote in an email. "He wanted us to sound better. Extended metaphors should be indulged and encouraged — the stranger, the better. And clichés were poison. 'Try harder,' he told me constantly. 'Create something with your own dirty little hands.' "

The curriculum's personal lessons were as rich as the pedagogical ones. "Don't raise your hand in class," he wrote. "This isn't Montessori, I expect people to speak up when they like, but don't speak over anyone."

"If you text or email during class, I will ignore you as you ignore me," David added. "It won't go well."

If his students did put in the effort, however, he made himself available.

"When class ended, it didn't mean that he went back to New York and stopped being our teacher," said Brooke Jackson-Glidden, 20, who credits being a student of David's with helping her secure her current spot in The Boston Globe's co-op program, something like an internship. "He understood that I cared about this," she added, "and that's all that really mattered to him."

David exuded confidence but was also humble. As he dove into his new job last fall, he acknowledged that the professor himself had a lot to learn. He cautioned the students that his classroom would be a work in progress.

"The good news is that this is the first time that I have taught this class, so boredom will not be an issue. It's also the bad news, because even though I have done a great deal of teaching over the years, it's the first time I've been an actual professor and have had to string together an entire semester. You are a beta, which means things will be exciting and sometimes very confusing. Let's be honest with each other when that happens. If you don't get where I am going or what I want, say so. I care deeply that I do a good job in all endeavors, especially this one."

The Legacy of Simeon Booker, a Pioneer of Civil Rights Journalism

OPINION | BY HOWARD W. FRENCH | DEC. 13, 2017

THE AFRICAN-AMERICAN JOURNALIST Simeon S. Booker Jr., who died this week at the age of 99, sensed an important story when Emmett Till, a black 14-year-old from Chicago, was lynched and mutilated during a summer visit to Mississippi in 1955 for supposedly flirting with a white woman.

Mr. Booker was then a reporter for the black-owned Johnson Publishing company. When Till's mother decided to hold an open-coffin funeral to reveal her son's almost unrecognizable face, he persuaded her to allow Johnson Publishing to photograph the corpse.

That image appeared in Jet magazine alongside an article by Mr. Booker and an earlier photograph of Till. It highlighted the savage brutality of American racism around the globe. The journalist and historian David Halberstam called it "the first great media event of the civil rights movement."

Jet was the country's only national newsmagazine for blacks, and it became a kind of social media for African-Americans in an era well before the internet. It was small in size, and therefore easily pocketable, circulating among family, friends and work mates. It carried word of black achievement, including news of independence sweeping across African countries, along with coverage of music, culture and beauty. The magazine celebrated black women in a way that would be incorrect today but provided relief from the suffocating omnipresence of white ideals. It would also carry an influential column by Mr. Booker from Washington on politics from a black perspective, called Ticker Tape U.S.A.

Over the next few years after the murder, Mr. Booker covered the sham trial and acquittal of Till's killers, the Birmingham bus boycotts, and then the desegregation of Central High School in Little Rock, Ark., achieved only through the presence of more than 1,000 Army paratroopers protecting nine black students from attack by howling white mobs. Based on this period alone, it would not be too much of an exaggeration to say that this singular figure founded civil rights reporting in American journalism. Yet his career covered six decades.

Simeon was the beloved nephew of my grandmother Dorothy W. Howard, or Nana, as I knew her and in whose house I grew up in northwest Washington. Civil rights activism ran in the family. A grandfather of hers, William Waring, was a freedman who worked in the Underground Railroad in Ohio and Michigan. Later, Nana would run a private integrated school in Washington, rare for its time, while Simeon's father ran a Y.M.C.A. that became a cornerstone of the black community in Baltimore. Simeon's second son, my cousin James Booker, who died in 1991, joined the Nation of Islam and changed his name to Abdul Wali Muhammad. He became editor in chief of the Nation's newspaper, The Final Call.

I guess I would have to say that journalism also ran in the family. Both Uncle Simeon and my older sister, Mary Ann, worked at The Washington Post. He worked there in the early 1950s and was their first African-American hire on the reporting staff. In my earliest days as a freelance reporter for that paper in Africa in the 1980s, I can remember Nana's excitement over my bylines, which she would share with Simeon, a legendary figure in Washington journalism by that point.

The story that I associate most vividly with this man comes from the 1960s. In my memories I see the bespectacled, often bow-tied Simeon shaking his head in living room conversations among elders, speaking gravely one moment and looking almost bemused the next as he recounted the terror that he experienced after entering Alabama aboard a Trailways bus as a reporter covering the Freedom Riders in 1961.

By that time, Simeon had become adept at all manner of survival tactics covering anti-black violence in the Deep South, whether it was moving by night to avoid detection, or carrying a well-worn Bible to pass himself off as a minister, or casting off his dapper bow ties and suits to dress as a sharecropper so as not to be seen as an "outside agitator." He escaped one angry white mob by stowing himself in the back of a hearse.

The Freedom Riders were protesting to oblige the government to enforce federal laws that prohibited segregation in interstate transport. Uncle Simeon was the only reporter to cover them, and that meant getting onto buses with the courageous black and white riders, all volunteers from the Congress of Racial Equality, and witnessing what happened as they purposely ignored the signs that indicated separate accommodations for whites and "colored."

In our household, in the Washington of the 1960s, civil rights were always the central topic of conversation. My father, a physician, had provided medical care during the historic 1965 civil rights march from Selma to Montgomery, Ala., and the following year both of my parents had done the same during the March Against Fear, from Memphis to Jackson, Miss.

It was Simeon who usually had the best stories, though, and his Freedom Riders experience has always chilled me deepest. At an Alabama rest stop, their driver returned to the bus, ashen faced, to announce that the other vehicle, which was slightly ahead of them, had been set on fire by a mob. Minutes later, seven rough-looking white men boarded Simeon's bus and began savagely beating the Freedom Riders. Simeon sat near the back, in the nominally black section, watching the scene through a hole he'd punched in a newspaper, trying amid the bloody frenzy to get a fix on some of the attackers so that he could describe them to the F.B.I.

The bus soon proceeded to Birmingham with the thugs aboard, whereupon its occupants were badly beaten once again. Somehow Simeon got away. "I had recently interviewed the attorney general about the Kennedy administration's plans for enforcing civil rights in the South," my uncle told Southern Quarterly in a 2014 interview.

"When I mentioned that I would be accompanying the Freedom Riders and that they expected trouble in the South, he had casually invited me to call him if any problems arose. When we finally reached Birmingham, I didn't hesitate to make that call. Within hours it became very clear the only way we would make it out was with federal help, which Robert Kennedy provided."

It would be easy for the physical courage and heroism of this period to obscure other kinds of valor, and it would be wrong, too. As the Washington bureau chief for Jet, Simeon had an opera box seat on the slow march of progress in the politics of race in America. He attended high-level news conferences and powerful Washington parties, and conducted numerous interviews with presidents. He often used his long-running column as a forum for unvarnished coverage of discrimination. He felt it was his duty as an African-American reporter not to allow the white establishment any opportunity to proclaim ignorance about the true state of affairs in the nation.

In his 1964 book, "Black Man's America," he described an interview with Dwight Eisenhower shortly after he left office: "As I prepared to leave, Ike flashed his famous smile, extended his hand, then said: 'Tell me. You've been here 45 minutes and all you've asked me are questions about civil rights. Is that all you're interested in?' I answered, 'Well, Mr. President, you spoke out on other issues while you were president, but no one knew how you really felt about the major civil rights issues."

HOWARD W. FRENCH, the author of "Everything Under the Heavens: How the Past Helps Shape China's Push for Global Power," is a professor at the Columbia University School of Journalism and a former foreign correspondent for The New York Times.

In Final Column, Jamal Khashoggi Laments Dearth of Free Press in Arab World

BY JACEY FORTIN | OCT. 17, 2018

THE DISSIDENT SAUDI JOURNALIST Jamal Khashoggi disappeared after he walked into the Saudi Consulate in Istanbul just over two weeks ago, and evidence increasingly suggests he was brutally murdered.

But on Wednesday night, a new piece of his work — submitted by his assistant after he disappeared — was published by The Washington Post, for which Mr. Khashoggi worked as a columnist.

In just over 700 words, his column lamented the dearth of a free press in the Arab world, which he said "is facing its own version of an Iron Curtain, imposed not by external actors, but through domestic forces vying for power." He sought to promote the free exchange of ideas and information under the headline, "What the Arab world needs most is free expression."

Mr. Khashoggi's editor, Karen Attiah, wrote a preface to the column. She said she received the file from Mr. Khashoggi's translator and assistant a day after he was reported to be missing.

"The Post held off publishing it because we hoped Jamal would come back to us so that he and I could edit it together," Ms. Attiah wrote. "Now I have to accept: That is not going to happen. This is the last piece of his I will edit for The Post."

The column came amid reports of audio recordings suggesting that Mr. Khashoggi was met by his killers shortly after he walked into the consulate in Turkey on Oct. 2, and that his fingers were severed and he was beheaded.

Saudi officials have denied harming Mr. Khashoggi, but they have not provided evidence that he left the Saudi Consulate, or offered a credible account of what happened to him.

President Trump appeared to take Saudi officials' claims at face value, disregarding Turkish assertions that senior figures in the royal court had ordered his killing. The president told reporters on Wednesday that the United States had asked for copies of any audio or video evidence of Mr. Khashoggi's killing that Turkish authorities may possess — "if it exists."

In his column on Wednesday, Mr. Khashoggi wrote that government clampdowns on the press in the Arab world were sometimes met with little resistance.

"These actions no longer carry the consequence of a backlash from the international community," he said. "Instead, these actions may trigger condemnation quickly followed by silence."

In Saudi Arabia, Mr. Khashoggi once served as an adviser to and unofficial spokesman for the royal family. But after Crown Prince Mohammed bin Salman barred him from writing in the kingdom, he traveled to the United States. He reinvented himself as a prominent critic of the Saudi government — and of Crown Prince Mohammed in particular — and became a resident of Virginia.

On Oct. 2, he entered the Saudi Consulate in Istanbul to pick up a document he needed to get married. His fiancée was waiting outside. But Mr. Khashoggi never came out.

His column on Wednesday was reminiscent of ones he had written before, which often condemned human rights abuses in Saudi Arabia. He wrote that he had been reading a Freedom House report on political rights and civil liberties around the world, and it ranked most countries in the Arab world as "not free."

"As a result, Arabs living in these countries are either uninformed or misinformed," Mr. Khashoggi wrote. "They are unable to adequately address, much less publicly discuss, matters that affect the region and their day-to-day lives."

He wrote about the hopes that had been shattered across the Middle East after Arab Spring uprisings in 2011 failed in several countries. And he wrote about governments' efforts to imprison dissidents, block internet communication and censor the media.

He suggested the formation of a transnational media outlet — like Radio Free Europe, which was created by the United States government during the Cold War — that could be a platform for Arab writers, reporters and thinkers.

"We need to provide a platform for Arab voices," Mr. Khashoggi wrote.

"We suffer from poverty, mismanagement and poor education. Through the creation of an independent international forum, isolated from the influence of nationalist governments spreading hate through propaganda, ordinary people in the Arab world would be able to address the structural problems their societies face."

In her note, Ms. Attiah wrote that Mr. Khashoggi's column "perfectly captures his commitment and passion for freedom in the Arab world. A freedom he apparently gave his life for."

MATT STEVENS contributed reporting.

How Two Times Reporters Pieced Together Allegations Against Ryan Adams

TIMES INSIDER | BY ALEXANDRIA SYMONDS AND KATIE VAN SYCKLE | FEB. 21, 2019

A recent report about alleged misconduct by the singer-songwriter took Joe Coscarelli and Melena Ryzik almost five months of reporting and hundreds of phone calls, meetings, texts and emails with more than two dozen sources.

Times Insider delivers behind-the-scenes insights into how news, features and opinion come together at The New York Times.

FOR NEARLY FIVE MONTHS, Joe Coscarelli and Melena Ryzik, culture reporters for The New York Times, collected accounts from dozens of sources, who detailed troubling behavior by Ryan Adams, the Grammy Award-nominated singer-songwriter. They outlined a spectrum of inappropriate acts, including emotional abuse of romantic partners and explicit text-message and video-chat exchanges with a minor Mr. Adams never met in person.

In response to The Times's investigation, several high-profile artists who had worked with Mr. Adams reacted online.

Karen Elson, the model and musician, wrote on Instagram, "I also had a traumatizing experience with Ryan Adams." (She later deleted the post.) Todd Wisenbaker, a guitarist who has worked extensively with Mr. Adams, posted a statement on Instagram with the caption: "This is incredibly hard for me to do, but Ryan, please get help." The pop star Mandy Moore, who was once married to Mr. Adams, repeated her own allegations against him on Marc Maron's "WTF" podcast.

"We've seen a number of musicians or people who are in that world say, yes, I've had a bad experience with Ryan Adams," said Ms. Ryzik. In the days since the article ran on Feb. 13, the reporters said they have received at least a dozen additional direct tips.

On Feb. 14, the F.B.I. opened an inquiry into whether Mr. Adams's communications with the underage fan constitute a crime. Through his lawyer, he has denied the allegations.

Mr. Coscarelli and Ms. Ryzik started their reporting after two nearly simultaneous events early last October: a discussion with a source who alluded to misconduct by a musician who turned out to be Mr. Adams, and an anonymous tip delivered through The Times's tip line that suggested looking into his treatment of women.

Mr. Coscarelli and Ms. Ryzik reached out to women known to have dated or otherwise been associated with Mr. Adams — touring with him as a supporting act, for example.

With the women who had firsthand experiences and decided that they may want to come forward as sources, "the initial interview was always an hour and a half long, at a minimum," Ms. Ryzik said.

Over the next few months, they were in contact with those women multiple times, making several trips to Los Angeles and Ohio to speak with them in person. In some cases, sources put them in touch with other women who had stories to share. There were, Mr. Coscarelli said, "many official interviews and then hundreds of texts, emails, check-ins, quick phone calls." In the days after publication, Ms. Ryzik estimated that she had texted with Ms. Moore six times.

As they listened to the women's experiences and gathered corroborating information from other sources, they discovered certain patterns of behavior. In relationships, Mr. Adams could be controlling: insisting that one partner, the musician Phoebe Bridgers, prove her whereabouts, for example, and threatening suicide if a woman didn't respond to his messages immediately. In the case of the young woman who was a teenager when she developed a texting relationship with Mr. Adams, several details stuck out as especially disturbing: video calls on Skype in which he exposed himself; nicknames for her body parts.

Mr. Coscarelli and Ms. Ryzik have worked on several articles about sexual abuse, separately and together. One thing they've learned about addressing such a delicate subject is that the women involved know their experiences best. "They know what the most damaging and damning parts of their accounts are," Ms. Ryzik said. "If something sticks out to them as, 'This really shows what the problem is,' then that's the kind of detail that you want in the story."

It has been more than 500 days since The New York Times published its first article detailing the film producer Harvey Weinstein's yearslong record of sexual harassment and assault allegations. The reporting set off a sea change both for Mr. Weinstein, who was arrested last May and is awaiting trial, and for culture at large. The #MeToo movement has unseated titans in industries including media, restaurants, politics and business, in many cases as a direct result of Times reporting that has continued to expose abuses of power and created ripple effects for those involved.

One reason Mr. Coscarelli and Ms. Ryzik, as well as their editors, Caryn Ganz and Ian Trontz, felt the Ryan Adams story was important to tell was it provided a window into the complicated power arrangements that undergird the world of pop music. "The music industry isn't like Hollywood; it doesn't operate in the same kind of power structure," Ms. Ganz said. "An artist can wield just as much power as a large executive; it's just a matter of their influence and connections."

Mr. Coscarelli said the Ryan Adams case is an example of a complex spectrum of behavior that includes subtler abuses of power that have been harder to document — but are much more common.

"I think as we're moving into Year 2 of #MeToo reporting, often it's not the R. Kellys and the Harvey Weinsteins of the world," he said, referring to two men who have been accused of rape or sexual abuse by many women, "but people who are abusing their power in more complex, but equally pernicious ways."

ALEXANDRIA SYMONDS is a senior staff editor at The Times.

KATIE VAN SYCKLE is a senior staff editor at The Times.

CHAPTER 6

Press Freedoms in the Trump Era

Declarations of "fake news" have become a catchphrase for President Trump. The Trump administration has launched an unprecedented assault on the press, often targeting The New York Times as a specific source of false reporting. His portrayal of the media as a direct adversary to his agenda has politicized the very nature of journalism, as he calls truth into question.

Where Will Trump Stand on Press Freedoms?

COLUMN | BY JIM RUTENBERG | NOV. 13, 2016

IT WAS MID-JUNE, and relations between Donald J. Trump and the news media had taken another dreadful turn. He had already vowed to change the libel laws to make it easier to sue journalists, and his personal insults were becoming more vicious. (One news correspondent was a "sleaze"; another was "third rate.")

Most troubling was that he was keeping a blacklist of news organizations he was banning from his rallies, and it was growing.

I called him at the time, to see what this would look like in a Trump administration. Would he deny White House credentials to select reporters and news organizations?

No, he said. "There, I'm taking something away, where I'm representing the nation."

STEPHEN CROWLEY/THE NEW YORK TIMES

Donald J. Trump traveled separately from reporters during his campaign. Now many Americans are wondering how the president-elect will treat press freedoms.

We can only hope he means it. Because if Mr. Trump keeps up the posture he displayed during the campaign — all-out war footing — the future will hold some very grim days, not just for news reporters but also for the American constitutional system that relies on a free and strong press.

It's one thing to wage a press war as a candidate, when the most you can do is enforce reporting bans at your rallies, hurl insults and deny interviews and access (all of which are plenty bad).

It's another thing to do it from 1600 Pennsylvania Avenue, where you have control over what vital government information is made public, and where you have sway over the Justice Department, which under President Obama has shown an overexuberance in investigating journalists and the whistle-blowers who leak to them.

Imagine what somebody with a press vendetta and a dim view of the First Amendment would do with that kind of power.

For their part, American newsrooms are conducting their own reassessments, vowing to do a better job covering the issues that animated his supporters, and acknowledging that Mr. Trump tapped into something in the national mood, the power of which they failed to grasp.

They now know they underestimate him again at their own peril. Yet they also know that the need to continue with probing, unflinching reporting that promotes the truth in the face of whatever comes at them will be great.

In the days immediately after Mr. Trump's victory, journalists that don't work at organizations with Breitbart in their names were preparing for potential reporting challenges, the likes of which they have never seen, while lawyers were gaming out possible legal strategies should Mr. Trump move against press freedoms.

Right after his victory Mr. Trump was telegraphing a gentler tone, declaring to The Wall Street Journal, "It's different now." Perhaps he was making his long-promised "pivot" to become "more presidential than anybody" save Abraham Lincoln.

But then came the Saturday night release of his "60 Minutes" interview in which he said he would keep his Twitter account so that when any news organization gave him "a bad story," he would "have a method of fighting back."

And he didn't skip a beat on Sunday morning, when he attacked The New York Times with a Twitter post that read, "Wow, the @nytimes is losing thousands of subscribers because of their very poor and highly inaccurate coverage of the 'Trump phenomena.' "

The statement was false. The paper said Sunday that postelection cancellations were so substantially outstripped by a surge of new subscriptions that its subscription growth rate in the period that followed Tuesday's result was four times the growth rate in the same period of last quarter.

In an atmosphere in which it's not shocking to hear about anti-Semitic literature being sent to the home of a Jewish reporter — the address having been published online by supporters of Mr. Trump — it was hard to see any of this as very presidential, though the definition may be changing.

The funny thing is that few major political figures have had a more codependent and at times friendly relationship with the press than Mr. Trump. Before he stopped doing news briefings in the later phase of the campaign, he was shaping up to be the most accessible major-party nominee in modern history.

But displeasing him could have an intensely personal cost, which the Fox News anchor Megyn Kelly vividly recalls in her new book, "Settle for More."

Ms. Kelly, who became Mr. Trump's leading television nemesis during the primary campaign, writes about how the candidate, unhappy with a segment she did in July 2015, threatened to unleash "my beautiful Twitter account against you."

After enduring her tough questioning at the first presidential primary debate, he made good on his Twitter promise, which in turn led to death threats against her, she said. ("I would spend many days of the coming months accompanied by security," she writes.) It didn't help, she wrote, that Mr. Trump's special counsel, Michael Cohen, recirculated a Trump supporter's tweet that read "we can gut her."

That was followed by what she took as another threat, from Mr. Trump's campaign manager at the time, Corey Lewandowski. As Mr. Lewandowski unsuccessfully lobbied a senior Fox News executive to remove Ms. Kelly from the next Fox debate, she writes, he said he would hate to see her go through such a "rough couple of days" again. (Fox News described the conversation the same way earlier this year.)

Mr. Lewandowski had been the living embodiment of Mr. Trump's aggressive approach to the press. He was, after all, arrested on charges that he manhandled the former Breitbart News reporter Michelle Fields. (Prosecutors in Florida ultimately dropped the charges.)

After a paid stint at CNN, Mr. Lewandowski returned to the Trump fold last week, and could wind up in the administration or at the Republican Party headquarters.

Another member of Mr. Trump's transition team, the Silicon Valley investor Peter Thiel, broke new ground this year by financing the "Hulk Hogan" lawsuit against Gawker, which resulted in Gawker's bankruptcy and sale to Univision.

Though that was technically an invasion-of-privacy case, it was a model for what Mr. Trump has said he wants to see in opening up libel laws.

Most First Amendment lawyers agree that fundamentally changing the libel law would require a reversal of the landmark Supreme Court case New York Times v. Sullivan. And while that might seem like a long shot, Laura R. Handman, a First Amendment lawyer, said in an interview that Mr. Trump could find ways to "chip away" at it.

First Amendment lawyers are more immediately concerned with potential leak investigations, as well as Freedom of Information Act requests, which can provide the best way to expose government secrets.

Look no farther than the potential attorney general candidate Rudolph W. Giuliani, who as mayor of New York was so allergic to records requests that news organizations and others regularly sued him for basic information.

Success at court was meaningless given that proceedings kept the information out of public view for so long that "he really won," said George Freeman, who was the assistant general counsel for The New York Times then and is now the executive director of the Media Law Resource Center.

I've said it before, but the solution will be what it has always been — good, tough reporting.

For all the appropriate discussion about how they missed some key dynamics of the race, mainstream news outlets produced a lot of top-flight journalism. They provided a glimpse into the tax returns Mr.

Trump wouldn't share; showed how he and Mrs. Clinton ran their charities; investigated their family business dealings; and bluntly called out falsehoods, more of which came from Mr. Trump.

The wrong lesson to take from the past year is that reporters should let up in their mission of reporting the truth, wherever it leads.

That's more important than ever, given how adept Mr. Trump and his allies have proved to be at promoting conspiracy theories that can spread faster than ever through social media.

But if there is one thing we learned this year, it was the wisdom of the old mnemonic device for the spelling of "assume" (makes an "ass" out of "u" and "me"). Mr. Trump campaigned through surprise and may well govern through surprise. We'll know how this thing is going to go only when we know.

Now, where's my seatbelt?

JIM RUTENBERG writes the Mediator column for The New York Times.

Billionaires vs. the Press in the Era of Trump

BY EMILY BAZELON | NOV. 22, 2016

A small group of superrich Americans — the president-elect among them — has laid the groundwork for an unprecedented legal assault on the media. Can they succeed?

IN 2005, TIM O'BRIEN, then a financial reporter at The New York Times, published the book "TrumpNation: The Art of Being the Donald." O'Brien talked to sources with an up-close view of Donald J. Trump's finances, who concluded that the real-estate developer's net worth was $150 million to $250 million, rather than the $2 billion to $5 billion Trump had variously claimed. Trump, who had courted O'Brien by taking him for rides in his Ferrari and private jet, sued O'Brien for libel in New Jersey in 2006. Trump called O'Brien a "wack job" on the "Today" show — while, O'Brien says, continuing to curry favor with him privately. O'Brien's publisher, Warner Books, was also named in the suit and hired top lawyers who put Trump through an unsparing two-day deposition. Asked about his finances, Trump was caught lying or exaggerating 30 times. "He thought he'd get a friendly judge, and we would roll over," says O'Brien, who is now the executive editor of Bloomberg View. "We didn't." The case went through four judges and was dismissed in 2009.

Trump's suit against O'Brien is one of seven forays President-elect Trump and his companies have made as libel plaintiffs. He won only once, when a defendant failed to appear. But the standard measure — defending his reputation and achieving victory in court — isn't how Trump says he thinks about his investment. "I spent a couple of bucks on legal fees, and they spent a whole lot more," he told The Washington Post in March about the hefty sum he spent on the case against O'Brien. "I did it to make his life miserable, which I'm happy about."

Trump was wrong: Warner Books spent less than he did, and O'Brien paid nothing. But that doesn't make Trump's central idea any less jarring: that libel law can be a tool of revenge. It's disconcerting for a superrich (if maybe not as rich as he says) plaintiff to treat the legal system as a weapon to be deployed against critics. Once installed in the White House, Trump will have a wider array of tools at his disposal, and his record suggests that, more than his predecessors, he will try to use the press — and also control and subdue it.

As a candidate, Trump blustered vaguely that he wanted to "open up our libel laws." I asked his spokeswoman, Hope Hicks, by email what he meant by that, but she didn't answer the question (or others I posed). It's not within the president's direct powers to change the rules for libel suits. But our legal safeguards for writers and publishers aren't foolproof. In the last few years, Trump has been joined by at least two billionaires who are determined to exploit cracks in the wall of defense around the press. The members of this club are innovators. They have sued or funded suits to defend reputations or protect privacy. But an underlying aim appears to be to punish critics like O'Brien or even destroy entire media outlets.

This kind of manipulation of the law is unfolding at a keen moment of weakness for the press, which has already been buffeted by falling revenue and mounting public disaffection. Only 40 percent of the public — the lowest rate since at least the 1990s — trusts the media "to report the news fully, accurately and fairly," according to a Gallup survey conducted in September 2015. This mistrust has been growing for a long time, but it was stoked by Trump during the campaign. He called the reporters who covered him "scum" and whipped up yelling and booing crowds. There is no consensus among his supporters that the press should hold those in power accountable. A recent Pew survey found that only half of Trump backers agreed that it was important in a strong democracy that "news organizations are free to criticize political leaders."

Media outlets have won many cases by persuading a judge to dismiss them. But since 2010, they have succeeded in only 39 percent of the libel and privacy suits that have gone to trial, a dip from 52 percent in the previous decade, according to the Media Law Resource Center. The median damage award has increased fivefold since the 1980s, to $1.1 million. The figure includes three big verdicts over the last eight months, against Gawker, Rolling Stone and The News & Observer in Raleigh, N.C. These include run-of-the-mill libel suits, and it's too early to say that the sky is falling on the press. But it's darkening.

THE HIGH BAR for winning a libel case in the United States was set in 1964, when the Supreme Court decided New York Times v. Sullivan. In that case, widely hailed as one of the court's strongest stands for free speech, L.B. Sullivan, a city commissioner who supervised the police in Montgomery, Ala., sued The Times over an ad in the newspaper signed by 100 civil rights supporters. The ad turned out to include minor factual errors. Sullivan said its depiction of how the Montgomery police responded to civil rights protests made him look bad. Under the rules at the time, a libel plaintiff was entitled to victory if he could show that the content that harmed his reputation was false. The Alabama jury agreed with Sullivan on that point and awarded him $500,000 in damages (the equivalent of about $4 million today). With similar cases pending, The Times pulled its reporters out of Alabama.

But when the newspaper appealed to the Supreme Court, the justices threw out the Sullivan verdict and set a far stiffer standard for proving libel. The court wrote that a public figure has to prove that a false and damaging statement about him was published with "actual malice," translated as "knowing or reckless disregard for the truth." By the 1980s, the number of libel suits decreased, and if suits did go to trial, they frequently ended in defeat for the plaintiff. In two examples from that era, Gen. William Westmoreland sued CBS, and Ariel Sharon, the Israeli defense minister, sued Time magazine. Neither man won damages. Those outcomes, as well as losses in other high-profile cases, "were a major deterrent for plaintiffs and their lawyers," says George Freeman, executive director of the Media Resource Law Center (and formerly a lawyer for The New York Times).

Superrich plaintiffs, however, aren't subject to the same market forces. They can treat suing the press as an investment, with the payoff being, at a minimum, the expense and time required for the other side to produce documents and sit for depositions. In February 2012, the magazine Mother Jones published a story about the Idaho billionaire Frank VanderSloot, a major donor to a "super PAC" that supported the Republican presidential candidate, Mitt Romney. In 1999, in response to a documentary, he sponsored billboards that asked, "Should public television promote the homosexual lifestyle to your children?" The magazine wrote that VanderSloot "outed" a gay reporter, Peter Zuckerman, and "bashed" Zuckerman and his reporting after he helped break a story in 2005 about a history of pedophilia by a Boy Scouts camp counselor in Idaho Falls. The portrayal of VanderSloot was based partly on several ads that he placed in The Idaho Falls Post Register. VanderSloot was upset at the story's implications for the Boy Scouts, and the ads called Zuckerman a "homosexual" and attacked him for having "a personal ax to grind."

VanderSloot sued Mother Jones for libel over the article. "They wanted to give me a public beating because I made a sizable donation to Mitt Romney," he told me. VanderSloot, who owns an online health-shopping club, also said the Mother Jones article cost him customers.

Over three years of proceedings, which included turning over internal emails, Mother Jones racked up about $2.5 million in legal fees. Insurance didn't cover the whole cost. "The suit was a huge drain on us," Clara Jeffery, editor in chief of the magazine, told me. "We're still digging our way out."

Judge Darla Williamson finally threw out VanderSloot's suit in October 2015, finding that Mother Jones's statements about him were either substantially true or opinions protected by the First Amendment. But Williamson took the unusual step of including a section in her opinion partially supporting his underlying complaint, accusing the magazine of "mudslinging" rather than recognizing its approach as squarely within the tradition of investigative journalism. Despite his defeat, VanderSloot declared himself "absolutely vindicated" and announced that he was creating a "Guardian of True Liberty Fund" to aid other people who want to sue the "liberal press." The fund has grown to between $1 million and $2 million, he told me, with five times that amount pledged, so that "as soon as something hits we think is worth it, we can go after it."

IT WAS ANOTHER BILLIONAIRE, Peter Thiel, who realized the full potential of bankrolling other people's lawsuits. Thiel, an influential figure in Silicon Valley who was a founder of PayPal and sits on the board of Facebook, is now an adviser to Donald Trump. Thiel and other Silicon Valley executives were regular targets of Gawker's aggressive reporting and mockery. In 2007, the site ran an article titled "Peter Thiel Is Totally Gay, People." Thiel didn't sue on his own behalf. But he secretly paid a Hollywood lawyer, Charles Harder, at least $10 million to sue Gawker on behalf of a suite of plaintiffs. Neither Thiel or Harder will say how many suits Thiel funded, but Harder has filed at least five against the website and its writers and editors. (He also represents Melania Trump in a $150 million suit in the United States against the British tabloid The Daily Mail and a Maryland blogger for calling her an "escort.") When Thiel's role was revealed by Forbes magazine, Thiel said his goal was "less about revenge and more about specific deterrence." Asked in October about his secrecy, Thiel said, "Transparency would have turned it into this very different narrative" that "it's this billionaire trying to squash the First Amendment." (He declined to comment for this article.)

Last March, while Thiel's role remained hidden, one of the suits he funded went to trial in Florida. The plaintiff, the aging wrestler-entertainer Hulk Hogan, sued Gawker for violating his privacy by publishing a brief video clip in October 2012 that showed him having sex. Hogan, whose real name is Terry G. Bollea, testified that he was emotionally devastated. Yet when he learned of the existence of the sex tape seven months earlier, Hogan appeared on "TMZ Live," joking about having sex with "several brunettes."

It's common for judges to dismiss privacy suits when the plaintiff has encouraged news interest. In a preliminary ruling before trial, the Florida Court of Appeals said that Gawker posted the sex tape as part of an "ongoing public discussion," citing Hogan's appearance on "TMZ" and later on "The Howard Stern Show." But Judge Pamela Campbell, who presided over the trial, instructed the jury to decide for itself whether the publication of the sex tape was "highly offensive to a reasonable person" and "not of legitimate concern to the public."

The jury seemed to channel the public's low regard for the press when they awarded Hogan $140 million in damages. "It just wasn't about punishment of these individuals and Gawker," one juror told ABC after the trial. "You had to do it enough where it makes an example in society and other media organizations." Within two months, Gawker's parent company declared bankruptcy. Gawker was sold and ceased publication.

In the half-century since New York Times v. Sullivan, the United States has often held itself up to the world as a beacon for the free press. American libel law, the theory goes, protects writers and publishers better than the laws of countries like Britain, where it's easier to win a libel judgment. Yet giant jury awards don't topple publications in the United Kingdom: The country has an unofficial damages cap of about £250,000 (plus legal fees). British publishers can, in essence, treat compensating someone whose reputation they have harmed as a cost of doing business. And it's less risky for them to apologize for a story that turns out to be wrong. "There are limits on damages for malpractice suits against doctors," says Robert Post, dean of the Yale Law School. "Why not for journalists?"

It's tempting to treat Gawker's demise as unique or deserved. But that's a false form of reassurance, a former editor of the site, Tom Scocca, argued in August. Every publication "is prepared to absorb the damage when it makes a mistake," he wrote on Gawker. "What Thiel's covert campaign against Gawker did was to invisibly change the terms of the risk calculation." The lesson, Scocca told his readers, is that "you live in a country where a billionaire can put a publication out of business."

What's new here are two forces squeezing journalism like pincers. The first is a figure like Thiel, willing to place bets on lawsuit after lawsuit until he hits on a winning combination of facts, judge and jury. The second is the public's animosity toward the press, now fueled by the soon-to-be president. Juries tend to reflect public sentiment and have recently penalized not just an irreverent new-media site like Gawker, but also a newspaper doing investigative work. In September, The News & Observer, which is more than 100 years old, went to trial over a libel claim brought by a former state ballistics agent in North Carolina, who sued regarding two articles from 2010 that included suspicions, by independent firearms experts, that she had falsified evidence to help prosecutors win a murder trial. The agent said that the suspicions were untrue and that she was effectively being accused of a crime. The News & Observer stands by its reporting. But the jury found against the paper and ordered it to pay about $9 million; the amount exceeded the state's cap on damages and is likely to be lowered to $6 million. The News & Observer plans to appeal.

IN THE WEEK BEFORE THE ELECTION, Seth Stevenson, a writer for Slate, followed the Trump campaign, which meant sitting in the pen where reporters were confined at rallies. He realized that the pen's function was to turn the press into a prop. "Behold," he imagined Trump saying to his fans. "I've rounded up a passel of those elites you detest. And I've caged them for you!"

Trump has continued to treat the press as a prop, or a punching bag, since his election. The weekend after his victory, he railed against The New York Times on Twitter for its "poor and highly inaccurate coverage of the 'Trump phenomena.'" Trump thrives on media attention, but it's also clear that as the press sinks in the public's estimation, any tough coverage of him will come to seem less credible. The media also serves as an all-purpose receptacle for blame. Asked on "60 Minutes" why African-Americans, immigrants and Muslims have expressed fear of his presidency, Trump didn't reckon with any of his own statements. He said, "I think it's built up by the press."

Whatever Trump's feelings about the media, New York Times v. Sullivan will surely survive his presidency. The case is revered, and in the last several years, the Supreme Court has moved to expand, not contract, the reach of the First Amendment. And states have taken steps, too: To prevent people from using the courts, and the discovery process, to silence or retaliate against their critics, 28 states and the District of Columbia have enacted anti-Slapp laws — the acronym stands for "strategic lawsuit against public participation." It's possible, however, that Trump could appoint judges who would find a way around the usual press protections. More immediately, he could ask his Justice Department to prosecute journalists who report leaks from his administration. (President Obama's Justice Department investigated reporters, but didn't charge them.) It's also possible that the press will be a meeker watchdog because of subtler changes that are harder to track. As the head of the executive branch, the president exerts a great deal of control over access to information. Federal agencies have power to shape the state of the union; they also describe it for us by producing reams of facts and statistics, which in turn shape our assessment of our elected leaders. Trump could hire people who cancel funding for government reports or research that doesn't serve his interests, or who suppress findings the administration doesn't like.

The new president will be a man who constantly accuses the media of getting things wrong but routinely misrepresents and twists facts himself. “Their single goal will be to burnish their reputation,” Tim O’Brien predicts of the Trump administration. There are signs, too, of new efforts to harness the law to the cause of cowing the press. Trump’s choice for chief adviser, Stephen Bannon, ran the alt-right Breitbart News Network before joining Trump’s campaign last summer. Breitbart announced last week that it was “preparing a multimillion-dollar lawsuit against a major media company” for calling Breitbart a “‘white nationalist’ website.” Even if Breitbart is bluffing, the threat will discourage other news outlets from using that term to describe it, and that will in turn help Breitbart and Bannon seem more acceptable to the mainstream. Trump was right about one thing: You don’t have to win every case to advance in the larger legal war.

EMILY BAZELON is a staff writer for the magazine and the Truman Capote fellow at Yale Law School.

Trump Is Damaging Press Freedom in the U.S. and Abroad

OPINION | BY JOEL SIMON | FEB. 25, 2017

SPEAKING AT THE Conservative Political Action Conference Friday, President Trump took his anti-media rhetoric to a new level, doubling down on his description of journalists as "the enemy of the people" and calling for an end to the use of anonymous sources. This on a day when his press secretary Sean Spicer barred reporters from The New York Times, BBC, BuzzFeed News, CNN, Politico, The Los Angeles Times and The Huffington Post from his daily White House press briefing.

The unrelenting attacks on the news media damage American democracy. They appear to be part of a deliberate strategy to undermine public confidence and trust by sowing confusion and uncertainty about what is true. But they do even greater damage outside the United States, where America's standing as a global beacon of press freedom is being drastically eroded.

This is not just a matter of United States prestige. At a time when journalists around the world are being killed and imprisoned in record numbers, Mr. Trump's relentless tirades against "fake news" are emboldening autocrats and depriving threatened and endangered journalists of one of their strongest supporters — the United States government.

Of course the United States' record on press freedom is far from perfect. During the Obama administration, aggressive leak investigations — including a record number of prosecutions under the 1917 Espionage Act — regularly ensnared the press. But the United States has had tremendous moral influence when it spoke out about press freedom violations, and not just because of the commitment to the First Amendment. The fact that United States political leaders regularly withstood relentless criticism in the press gave them legitimacy when they called for the protection of critical voices in repressive societies.

DOUG MILLS/THE NEW YORK TIMES

White House press secretary Sean Spicer clapped as President Trump spoke at the Conservative Political Action Conference on Friday.

For example, the Obama administration, through public statements and behind-the-scenes diplomacy, helped win the release of imprisoned journalists in Ethiopia and Vietnam. President George W. Bush regularly spoke out about press freedom violations, in places like Venezuela and Zimbabwe.

Earlier this month, the Venezuelan government suspended CNN's Spanish language network following accusations by President Nicolás Maduro that the network manipulates the news. President Trump was silent. Really, what could he say?

More ominously, when Mr. Trump was asked in December to comment on the systematic killings of journalists in Russia, he shrugged. "Well I think our country does plenty of killing, too," he told MSNBC's Joe Scarborough.

So far, Mr. Trump's war on the media has been mostly a war of words. But those words have consequences. It is leaders of autocratic countries, not democracies, who make a point of telling journalists how they should do their job. Praising positive coverage while lashing out at reporters who write something critical gives succor to the likes of President Recep Tayyip Erdogan of Turkey, a country where news outlets have been shuttered and a record number of journalists imprisoned. Meanwhile, Mr. Trump's attacks on the use of anonymous sources undermine the work of journalists reporting sensitive stories in repressive and dangerous environments from Iraq to Mexico, where source protection is a matter of life and death.

Mr. Trump's attacks on the news media follow a political logic. They rally those among his supporters who despise the media for its perceived liberal bias; they erode the credibility of the media itself, undermining demands for accountability; and they serve as the ultimate distraction, in the most recent example deflecting public attention from reports that Trump administration officials are impeding the investigation into their ties to Russia.

Thus there is a risk that responding to Mr. Trump's provocations will further advance his aims. Still, one point must be made: In President Trump's carpet bombing of the news media, it is not just the United States' global reputation that is collateral damage. Rather, it is the brave journalists on the front line who risk their lives and liberty to bring the world the news. It is to our great shame that they can no longer count on the support of the United States.

JOEL SIMON is the executive director of the Committee to Protect Journalists.

Amid Leaks, Recalling an Epic Battle Over Press Freedom in Nixon Era

RETRO REPORT | BY CLYDE HABERMAN | MARCH 26, 2017

Retro Report re-examines the leading stories of decades past.

AS DETAILS TRICKLED into print and pixels about Russian tampering with the election that put him in the White House, a snappish President Trump lashed out in his favored medium. On Feb. 15, he wrote on Twitter: "The real scandal here is that classified information is illegally given out by 'intelligence' like candy. Very un-American!"

No need to consider here the confectionery metaphor or the denigration of information-gathering agencies implied by his wrapping "intelligence" in quotation marks. On the matter of divulging government material, though, history strongly suggests that a more accurate tweet would have been: "Very American!"

Leaked information — its uses and abuses — lies at the heart of the current episode of Retro Report, a series of essays and video documentaries that study major news stories of the past and how they influence events today. Presidents themselves have long encouraged seepage when it suits their purposes, as the New York Times columnist James Reston observed decades ago. "The ship of state," he said, "is the only known vessel that leaks from the top." It is when unauthorized disclosures put them on the spot that leaders start wailing. This has been so since the earliest days of the republic.

President Barack Obama may have publicly extolled the virtues of a free press, but his government pressed criminal charges against more people for news leaks than all previous administrations combined. Rhetorically, anyway, Mr. Trump has raised the temperature many more degrees by declaring the news media to be nothing less than the enemy of the people, a phrase more familiar coming from the likes of Stalin and other despots.

Retro Report's focus is an epic battle that started on June 13, 1971, when The Times published a secret government history of the Vietnam War that it labeled "Vietnam Archive." Soon enough, people began referring to it as the Pentagon Papers. The name stuck. Publication of this highly classified material, which had been given to the newspaper by a military analyst, Daniel Ellsberg, became a defining moment in government-press relations.

Across 7,000 pages, the papers detailed government deceit and evasion that had led the United States to stumble into a war that turned highly unpopular. No operational details relevant to the continuing war in 1971 were revealed.

"This was not a breach of national security," Arthur Ochs Sulzberger, The Times's president and publisher at the time, said then. "We gave away no national secrets. We didn't jeopardize any American soldiers or Marines overseas." (Mr. Sulzberger was himself a Marine who had served in World War II and the Korean War.)

Even though the revelations concerned events that occurred before he took office, President Richard M. Nixon was enraged. He rejected the notion that Americans deserved, almost by definition, to know how their leaders made life-or-death decisions.

Invoking national security, his administration demanded a halt to the papers' publication. The Times refused, citing the First Amendment. The government then obtained a temporary restraining order from a federal judge in Manhattan. It was the first time in United States history that a court, on national security grounds, had blocked a newspaper in advance from running a specific article — had exercised prior restraint, as it is called.

The case rapidly went to the Supreme Court. On June 30, in a 6-to-3 vote, the justices rejected the administration's arguments and upheld The Times's right to publish. There has been no other known instance since then of the government's seeking in court to prevent an American newspaper from printing secret information by raising a cry of national security, a phrase that Mr. Sulzberger felt was often abused.

"It's a wonderful way, if you've got egg on your face, to prevent anybody from knowing it: Stamp it secret and put it away," he said.

The Nixon administration certainly tried to put Mr. Ellsberg away. He was accused of, among other things, violating the Espionage Act of 1917. But the case against him and a co-defendant, Anthony J. Russo, fell apart with revelations of serious government misconduct, including illegal wiretapping, and the charges were dismissed.

For Mr. Ellsberg, who turns 86 on April 7, Nixon's dismissal of the public's right to know was "a mockery of a democracy."

"Can you really have democracy, in a real sense," he said to Retro Report, "with the government having the final voice and the total voice as to what citizens shall know about what they're doing, and whether they're telling the truth and whether they're obeying the law? I would say no."

Such questions have plainly not faded in this age of WikiLeaks and Edward J. Snowden and their revelations about government monitoring of United States citizens. Admirers often liken Mr. Snowden and the WikiLeaks founder, Julian Assange, to Mr. Ellsberg. These comparisons, however, would seem to stretch only so far. Mr. Ellsberg's goal was to change a particular government policy. He did not breach secrecy for the sake of breaching secrecy, as latter-day leakers have arguably done.

Then, too, many question whether Mr. Assange is truly committed to transparency or, rather, to finding information that he can weaponize. In the 2016 presidential campaign, he unloaded material intended to damage Hillary Clinton's candidacy. To more than a few people, it seemed an exercise less in shedding light than in settling scores with a former secretary of state he disliked.

Without leaks, Americans would have known considerably less — or nothing at all — about dubious actions taken in their name. To cite but a few examples: the abuse of detainees at the Abu Ghraib prison in Iraq, the warrantless monitoring of citizens' emails and phone calls by the National Security Agency, the clandestine sale of weaponry to the

Iranian government in what came to be called the Iran-contra affair, and the multi-tentacle Watergate scandal that forced Nixon to resign. More recently, the Panama Papers exposed a global system of tax evasion.

For a nervous bureaucrat, stamping "Secret" on a piece of paper can be a safer course than leaving it untouched and inviting unintended consequences. But more than four million government employees are cleared for access to classified material. This means no shortage of possibilities for Washington to turn into a giant colander.

Despite inherent tensions, a symbiosis between government and the news media has long been evident. Perhaps not surprisingly, and even given the Obama administration's relatively aggressive stance, instances of leakers' being hauled into the dock are rare.

And just because something is leaked, it is not necessarily compelling to everyone. Mr. Sulzberger, who died in 2012, attested to that in a speech that he gave in 1996, on the 25th anniversary of the release of the Pentagon Papers. Given that he risked being jailed for publishing them, he felt he should first examine them for himself, he said, but "until I read the Pentagon Papers, I did not know that it was possible to read and sleep at the same time."

Independent Press Is Under Siege as Freedom Rings

COLUMN | BY JIM RUTENBERG | JULY 2, 2017

HAPPY BIRTHDAY, America, I guess.

You're old enough to know that you can't always have a feel-good birthday. And let's face it: This Fourth of July just isn't going to be one of them. How could it be when one of the pillars of our 241-year-old republic — the First Amendment — is under near-daily assault from the highest levels of the government?

When the president of the United States makes viciously personal attacks against journalists — and then doubles down over the weekend by posting a video on Twitter showing himself tackling and beating a figure with a CNN logo superimposed on his head? (Every time you think he's reached the limit ...)

How could it be when the president lashes out at The Washington Post by making a veiled threat against the business interests of its owner, Jeff Bezos, suggesting that his other company, Amazon, is a tax avoider?

(Where have we seen that sort of thing before — Russia maybe?)

Or when the White House plays so many games with its press briefings, taking them off camera and placing conditions on how and when they can run — or, in the case of its rare, unrestricted live briefings, using them to falsely accuse the news media of "dishonesty"?

For those who cherish a robust free press, it's hard to feel much like partying after witnessing how some cheered Representative Greg Gianforte, Republican of Montana, for body slamming a reporter for The Guardian, Ben Jacobs. His sin: asking unwelcome questions.

The "he had it coming" camp's celebration of the violence against a reporter seemed out of step with Mr. Gianforte's own response. He ultimately apologized, pleaded guilty to assault and pledged a $50,000 donation to the Committee to Protect Journalists.

Then again, it wasn't out of step with President Trump, whose weekend tweet appeared to promote violence against CNN — which, some argued, violated Twitter's harassment policies — certainly undercut Mr. Gianforte's message of contrition.

Yes, America, all of the attacks against something so central to your identity must have you in quite the birthday funk.

The likely reaction in anti-press precincts to a column like this one will be that mainstream journalists think they're above reproach, which is nonsense.

When a real news organization makes a mistake, it takes action, as CNN recently did when it retracted an article about the Russia investigation, saying the article had not received the proper vetting. Three people lost their jobs.

The Trump administration torqued it into supposed proof that CNN and much of the rest of the news media — including The New York Times and The Washington Post — are "fake news."

It was a powerful reminder to journalists everywhere to take the extra time to get it right, to make sure that the processes that ensure editorial quality and accuracy remain intact and strong.

The stakes are higher now, as the anti-press sentiment veers into calls for more action against journalists, if not against journalism itself.

Look no further than the new National Rifle Association advertisement. In it, the conservative radio and television star Dana Loesch angrily describes how "they" — whoever they are — "use their media to assassinate real news," contributing to a "violence of lies" that needs to be combated with "the clenched fist of truth."

Given that the ad was for a pro-gun group, this sort of thing "tends toward incitement," Charles P. Pierce wrote in Esquire. (Added context: The N.R.A. chief Wayne LaPierre recently called "academic elites, political elites and media elites" America's "greatest domestic threats.")

The Fox News host Sean Hannity has urged the Trump administration to force reporters to submit written requests in advance of the daily White House press briefing, which, he said, should be narrowly tailored to specific topics the administration wants to talk about.

Mr. Hannity's good buddy Newt Gingrich went one better, suggesting that administration officials fully close the briefing room to the news media, which he has called "a danger to the country right now."

What's most extraordinary in all of this is how many people calling for curtailments on the free press are such professed "constitutionalists" and admirers of the founders.

The founders didn't view the press as particularly enlightened, and from the earliest days of the republic it certainly wasn't. (To wit, a passage in The Aurora, an early publication, described George Washington as "the source of all the misfortunes of our country.")

But they drafted the founding documents to enshrine press freedom for good reason. As the Stanford University history professor Jack Rakove said in an interview last week, James Madison was most concerned about a misinformed public's acting on misplaced passions, and saw the press as an antidote. Were he alive now, Mr. Rakove said, "Madison would be worried by the idea of government whipping up or exploiting" what he called "badly formed passions."

Sure, there were the occasional stumbles, like the short-lived Alien and Sedition Acts of 1798, which banned "false, scandalous and malicious writing" about the government, but they led to stronger free speech protections.

So this, our 241st birthday, seems just the time to invite some of our forebears to remind us — including those at the top of the government — why a free press is so important.

"Whoever would overthrow the liberty of a nation must begin by subduing the freeness of speech." — **Benjamin Franklin**, 1722

"There is nothing so fretting and vexatious, nothing so justly terrible to tyrants, and their tools and abettors, as a free press." — **Samuel Adams**, 1768

"The freedom of speech may be taken away — and, dumb and silent we may be led, like sheep, to the slaughter." — **George Washington**, to officers of the Army, 1783

"Nothing could be more irrational than to give the people power, and to withhold from them information without which power is abused. A popular government, without popular information, or the means of acquiring it, is but a prologue to a farce or a tragedy; or, perhaps both." — **James Madison**, 1822

"There is a terrific disadvantage not having the abrasive quality of the press applied to you daily, to an administration. Even though we never like it, and even though we wish they didn't write it, and even though we disapprove, there still isn't any doubt that we couldn't do the job at all in a free society without a very, very active press." — **John F. Kennedy**, 1962

"Since the founding of this nation, freedom of the press has been a fundamental tenet of American life. There is no more essential ingredient than a free, strong and independent press to our continued success in what the founding fathers called our 'noble experiment' in self-government.' " — **Ronald Reagan**, 1983

"Power can be very addictive, and it can be corrosive. And it's important for the media to call to account people who abuse their power, whether it be here or elsewhere." — **George W. Bush**, 2017

JACLYN PEISER contributed reporting.

JIM RUTENBERG writes the Mediator column for The New York Times.

Trump Takes Aim at the Press, With a Flamethrower

COLUMN | BY JIM RUTENBERG | AUG. 23, 2017

EVERY TIME YOU THINK President Trump's anti-press rhetoric can't get worse, he finds a way of surprising you and not surprising you all at the same time.

That he will attack journalists on a regular basis should be expected at this point, and it is. The surprising part comes when he manages to outdo himself. After all, he couldn't possibly top "enemy of the people," could he?

Yet there he was in Phoenix on Tuesday, telling a crowd of thousands of ardent supporters that journalists were "sick people" who he believes "don't like our country," and are "trying to take away our history and our heritage."

The moment matters. Mr. Trump's latest attack on the media came at a time of heightened racial tension stoked by a white supremacists' rally in Charlottesville, Va., and continuing now in the national debate over removing statues that commemorate Confederate figures from the Civil War. Mr. Trump's speech in Phoenix reprised a question spawned by his raucous rallies during the presidential campaign: How long before someone is seriously hurt, or worse?

"Coming off the violence in Charlottesville, with tensions so high and the kindling so dry, it felt like President Trump was playing recklessly with fire, singling out a specific group of people — the media — for disliking America and trying to erase our country's heritage," Jim VandeHei, chief executive of the Axios news website, told me. "He's just wrong to paint so wildly with such a broad brush, and, worse, putting reporters at real risk of retribution or violence."

(In a passionate appeal on Twitter on Wednesday, Mr. VandeHei posted the following message: "To family/friends who support

DAMON WINTER/THE NEW YORK TIMES

Members of the media covering a campaign appearance by Donald J. Trump at a school in Council Bluffs, Iowa, before the state's Republican presidential caucuses last year.

Trump: What he said last night was despicable, extremely deceptive, dangerous.")

The president's remarks on Tuesday were diciest for the news organizations that he identified by name.

"When you see 15,000 people turn on your colleagues behind a rope, yeah, you worry about it," George Stephanopoulos, the chief anchor for ABC News, told me on Wednesday. Mr. Trump insulted Mr. Stephanopoulos personally in Phoenix while singling out his news organization.

As usual, CNN got the worst of it, facing chants that included "CNN Sucks," although ABC and CNN both reported that none of their personnel had been threatened physically.

I have to admit that I had started to wonder in the past few weeks what all the presidential inveighing against the news media was actually amounting to. For all of Mr. Trump's attacks, American journalists have continued their investigative digging, aggressive fact-checking and relentless reporting inside the administration, to impressive effect (See: Flynn, Michael; Trump, Donald Jr.; and, most recently, Icahn, Carl, among many other examples).

The anti-media rhetoric would become more ominous, I thought with a sense of dread, if, say, the Justice Department decided to issue subpoenas more freely in federal leak prosecutions to compel reporters to divulge their sources, as Attorney General Jeff Sessions has suggested it might.

But to dismiss Mr. Trump's rhetoric would be to disregard the risk of violence that comes with the kind of presidential incitement we saw Tuesday night.

It would also mean disregarding an element of presidential leadership that we are all taught in grammar school: its broad influence — how it can set a tone for others to follow.

Yes, mistrust of the media was growing even before Mr. Trump emerged on the political scene. But this much is unmistakable: The president is significantly adding to what is, without question, the worst anti-press atmosphere I've seen in 25 years in journalism, and real, chilling consequences have surfaced, not just in the United States, but around the world.

Look at how People's Daily of China disputed reports about the torture that the human rights lawyer Xie Yang said he had endured at the hands of government interrogators, calling it "Fake News," and how Cambodia threatened to expel foreign news organizations, including Voice of America and Radio Free Asia, because of Mr. Trump's assertions that reporters were dishonest.

"It's providing cover for repression around the world," said Courtney Radsch, the director for advocacy at the Committee to Protect Journalists.

The committee has generally focused on reporters abroad, but last month it started a new website, "U.S. Press Freedom Tracker," to monitor episodes involving journalists in this country. Its lead items on Wednesday were about attacks on journalists in Charlottesville from both white nationalists and counterprotesters aligned with the so-called antifa movement.

Financing for the site came partly from $50,000 that Representative Greg Gianforte, Republican of Montana, donated to the committee as part of his settlement with Ben Jacobs, a reporter for The Guardian whom Mr. Gianforte body-slammed this year when Mr. Jacobs approached him with questions. (Mr. Gianforte pleaded guilty to a misdemeanor assault charge in June.)

Some of the most disturbing moves against the press this year stem from a new brand of anti-media vigilantism. And this has been a particularly bad week for that, too.

Allow me to direct you to Martin Shkreli, whom a Brooklyn jury convicted this month of security fraud related to a stock scheme involving a pharmaceutical company he co-founded, Retrophin. But you probably know Mr. Shkreli from his company Turing Pharmaceuticals's outrageous increasing of prices on a drug that helps people with compromised immune systems fight parasitic infections.

On Wednesday, Business Insider reported that Mr. Shkreli was developing websites devoted to reporters at CNBC, Vice, Vanity Fair and several other organizations, filling them with politically tinged attacks. He said it was justified because, in his view, the subjects of his animosity didn't qualify as journalists.

Further cementing this week as a dark one for American journalism, a reporter at ProPublica, Julia Angwin, said on Twitter that an attack on her email account had rendered it inoperable. Similar attacks hit the reporters who worked with her on an article published over the weekend that detailed how major technology companies were facilitating the financing of groups identified as extremists by the Anti-Defamation League and the Southern Poverty Law Center.

The attacks on ProPublica were so intense that they caused the entire staff to lose access to incoming email for five or six hours on Tuesday, the journalism organization's president, Richard Tofel, told me.

"I assume something like this is designed to prevent these people from doing their jobs," he said. "And we have every intention to continue to do our jobs."

And that was the answer, of course; it has been all year, the year before that and so on.

"At some level," as Mr. Stephanopoulos told me, "that's all we can do."

He added: "You have to trust that if we do our job and do it well and do it with integrity and don't make mistakes, that in the end, the sort of fundamental idea behind the First Amendment — that the truth will out — will actually take place."

What seemed to particularly sting on Wednesday was the way that Mr. Trump had impugned journalists' patriotism.

"Claim bias. Fine. Claim elitism. Fine," Mr. VandeHei of Axios wrote on Twitter. "But to say reporters erase America's heritage, don't love America, turn off cameras to hide truth, are to blame for racial tension, is just plain wrong."

Anyone with a passing interest in history knows that the founders viewed an independent press as essential to democracy. Talk about heritage.

JIM RUTENBERG writes the Mediator column for The New York Times.

One Thing Donald Trump Would Like Is Freedom From the Press

OPINION | BY THOMAS B. EDSALL | MARCH 15, 2018

MORE THAN ANY president in living memory, Donald Trump has conducted a dogged, remorseless assault on the press. He portrays the news media not only as a dedicated adversary of his administration but of the entire body politic. These attacks have forced the media where it does not want to be, at the center of the political debate.

Trump's purpose is clear. He seeks to weaken an institution that serves to constrain the abusive exercise of executive authority. He has initiated a gladiatorial contest pitting the principle of freedom of the press against a principle of his own invention: freedom from the press.

Trump has his media favorites, Fox News and other organizations that serve as approved public relations outlets, versus the "fake news," meaning virtually everything else.

Politicians have frequently questioned the neutrality and objectivity of specific journalists, their stories and their publications, but Trump has raised the stakes to a new level. He has described news organizations as "the enemy of the American people." He has routinely called reporters "scum," "slime," "dishonest" and "disgusting."

In November, Trump proposed a contest to determine which network — Fox excluded — "is the most dishonest, corrupt and/or distorted in its political coverage of your favorite President (me). They are all bad. Winner to receive the FAKE NEWS TROPHY!"

The news media "have been incorporated into the political style of the governing party as fixed hate objects," Jay Rosen, a professor of journalism at N.Y.U., wrote in an email to me.

Rosen observed that the history of right-wing attacks on the media

> *extends back through Agnew's speeches for Nixon to Goldwater's campaign in 1964 and winds forward through William Rusher, talk radio, and of course Fox News, which founded a business model on liberal bias.*

There is an underlying strategy to Trump's critique of the media. Rosen continued:

> *Trump is not just attacking the press but the conditions that make it possible for news reports to serve as any kind of check on power. Trump is the apotheosis of this history and its accelerant. He has advanced the proposition dramatically. From undue influence (Agnew's claim) to something closer to treason (enemy of the people.) Instead of criticizing 'the media' for unfair treatment, he whips up hatred for it. Some of his most demagogic performances have been exactly that. Nixon seethed about the press in private. Trump seethes in public, a very different act.*

Trump has some built-in advantages in his war on the media. Confidence in the media was in decline long before Trump entered politics — a slide that reflected the rise in political polarization. Gallup reported in September 2017 that 37 percent of the public had a "great deal" or "fair amount" of confidence in the mass media, down from 53 percent in 1997. And Trump's critique of the media reaches a highly receptive audience.

An April 2017 Gallup survey found that by a margin of more than 2 to 1, the public said that the press favored one party over the other. Of those who said the media is partisan, 64 percent said that the media favors Democrats, and 22 percent said Republicans.

The media, on the other hand, enters the fray with significant disadvantages.

In a 2017 paper, "Enemy Construction and the Press," RonNell Andersen Jones and Lisa Grow Sun, law professors at the University of Utah and Brigham Young University, argue that Trump's goal is fundamentally malign:

> *The Trump administration, with a rhetoric that began during the campaign and burgeoned in the earliest days of Donald Trump's presidency, has engaged in enemy construction of the press, and the risks that accompany that categorization are grave.*

Insofar as Trump succeeds in "undercutting the watchdog, educator, and proxy functions of the press," they write, *it leaves the administration more capable of delegitimizing other institutions and constructing other enemies — including the judiciary, the intelligence community, immigrants, and members of certain races or religions.*

Jones and Sun contend that in many respects, Trump is reminiscent of Richard M. Nixon:

Nixon, like Trump, accused the media of being out to get him and predicted that the press would mischaracterize his public support or the reception he received. He believed the liberal media to be biased against him personally, maintaining that he had "entered the presidency with less support from the major publications and TV networks than any president in history" and that "their whole objective in life is to bring us down."

Unlike Trump, however, Nixon (like the country's founders)

routinely reaffirmed to both the press and the public that he conceived of the press as central to democracy. Indeed, in his first speech to the public regarding the Watergate scandal, Nixon acknowledged that "the system that brought the facts to light and that will bring those guilty to justice" was a system that included "a vigorous free press."

Trump stands out, according to Jones and Sun, in that his administration

has passed a threshold not approached by previous administrations in their tensions with the media. Trump is signaling — through his terminology, through his delegitimizing actions, and through his anticipatory undercutting — that the press is literally the enemy, to be distrusted, ignored, and excluded.

In response to my email, Jones replied that "war has been declared, whether they (the media) like it or not." She noted that the instincts of the press

motivate it to want to call out the changing norms that it sees around it, and to defend the role of important democratic institutions when they are attacked. But when the press is itself one of those institutions, it finds itself a part of the story in ways that it is unaccustomed to being, and it has to weigh the potential loss of credibility that might come with an aggressive self-defense.

I asked Jonathan Ladd, a professor of public policy and government at Georgetown, what strategies he thought the media should adopt to counter negative portrayals by conservatives.

"The best way for the press to react to Trump's undemocratic behavior is to continue trying to do their jobs the best they can," Ladd wrote. "The press is not perfect, but Trump's bad behavior doesn't change what they need to do."

Ladd specifically warned against "reacting to Trump by becoming more crusadingly anti-Trump."

Trump has successfully "put the mainstream media in a difficult position," according to Geoffrey Stone, a law professor at the University of Chicago:

If the media directly address the accusations of fake news, they ironically run the risk of dignifying the accusations. But if they ignore the accusations, they miss the opportunity to prove their professionalism to those who have grown skeptical.

In the long term, Stone suggested, we could begin to remedy this problem if we improved civic education and encouraged a stronger defense of the media by politicians, especially Republicans — a prospect about which he is not optimistic.

Of the media itself, however, Stone wrote:

I don't know that there's really much they can do to defend themselves. Those who trust them will continue to trust them. Those who distrust them are unlikely to be brought around by anything they themselves are likely to say.

Trump's disdain for the First Amendment is an integral part of a much longer series of developments in which both parties have demonstrated a willingness to defy democratic norms, although the Republican Party has been in the forefront.

In "Asymmetric Constitutional Hardball," Joseph Fishkin and David E. Pozen, law professors at the University of Texas and Columbia, write:

> *For a quarter of a century, Republican officials have been more willing than Democratic officials to play constitutional hardball — not only or primarily on judicial nominations but across a range of spheres. Democrats have also availed themselves of hardball throughout this period, but not with the same frequency or intensity.*

Fishkin and Pozen cite the work of Mark Tushnet, a professor at Harvard Law School, to define constitutional hardball as "political claims and practices"

> *that are without much question within the bounds of existing constitutional doctrine and practice but that are nonetheless in some tension with existing pre-constitutional understandings. Constitutional hardball tactics are viewed by the other side as provocative and unfair because they flout the 'goes without saying' assumptions that underpin working systems of constitutional government. Such tactics do not generally flout binding legal norms. But that only heightens the sense of foul play insofar as it insulates acts of hardball from judicial review.*

Republicans on the far right, in particular, Fishkin and Pozen write, have been willing to engage in constitutional hardball because they are drawn to "narratives of debasement and restoration," which suggest

> *that something has gone fundamentally awry in the republic, on the order of an existential crisis, and that unpatriotic liberals have allowed or caused it to happen.*

The severity of the liberal threat, in the eyes of these conservatives, justifies extreme steps to restore what they see as a besieged moral order.

In an email, Fishkin wrote:

> *As with so many things about President Trump, it strikes me that he*

> *didn't start the fire. He got into office because it was already burning and now he's pouring on gasoline.*

In Fishkin's view, Trump will do all he can to make the conflict between his party and the press "sharper and more intense, in the same way that he depends on and aims to intensify partisan polarization."

Pozen warned in an email:

> *Accusations that the press has a political agenda can, perversely, help create an agenda which is then said to corroborate the accusations.*

Pozen described Trump's denunciation of the press as "the culmination of several decades of comparable attacks by media pundits, such as Rush Limbaugh" and he argues that Trump's calls

> *to lock up one's general election opponent, encouraging online hate mobs, lying constantly, attacking the press constantly, contradicting oneself constantly, undermining the very idea of truth are individually and in common potentially profound threats to the integrity and quality of our system of free expression.*

The question is whether the news media can mount an effective check on the exercise of power when the media itself has become an object of hatred for a large segment of the electorate.

Rosen of N.Y.U. notes the cross pressures on the news media:

> *I think our top journalists are correct that if they become the political opposition to Trump, and see themselves that way, they lose. But they have to go to war against a political style in which power gets to write its own story.*

Rosen draws attention to a September 2017 article in The Atlantic, "Trump's War Against the Media Isn't a War: You need two sides for that," which quotes Marty Baron, executive editor of The Washington Post: "We're not at war; we're at work." Baron is right, but for those without any understanding of — or respect for — freedom of the press, first principles can be brushed aside without a second thought.

Crowds, Stoked by Trump's Rhetoric, Increase Their Ire Toward the Press

BY MICHAEL M. GRYNBAUM | AUG. 1, 2018

THE BABY WEARING a "CNN Sucks!" pin pretty much summed it up.

In the back of a fairground auditorium in Tampa, Fla., on Tuesday night, as President Trump presided over a rally dedicated to denigrating his enemies, the journalists dispatched to cover the proceedings attracted their own raucous crowd.

"Stop lying!" shouted a man in an American flag T-shirt, one of dozens of Trump supporters who hurled invective at the assembled press corps. Facing the reporters' work space — and away from the stage where Mr. Trump was set to speak — they flashed middle fingers and chanted "CNN Sucks!" as Jim Acosta, a CNN White House correspondent, attempted to speak on-air.

Menacing the media was a theme of Mr. Trump's campaign rallies in 2016. News networks hired security guards for some correspondents — a practice that, in Mr. Acosta's case, has continued — and reporters found themselves taunted and disparaged by attendees repeating Mr. Trump's refrain of "fake news."

In Tampa, though, several journalists described an atmosphere of hostility that felt particularly hard-edge. And far from condemning these attacks on the press, the president and his team have endorsed them.

That night, Mr. Trump tweeted out a video of his supporters jeering Mr. Acosta, along with an approving comment from his son Eric: "#truth." When the White House press secretary, Sarah Huckabee Sanders, was invited at Wednesday's press briefing to condemn the menacing behavior, she declined.

"While we certainly support freedom of the press," Ms. Sanders said, "we also support freedom of speech. And we think that those things go hand in hand."

Now, news organizations are anticipating an unnerving autumn, as their reporters prepare to fan out across the country for a fresh round of Trump rallies before the midterm elections. "I'll go six or seven days a week when we're 60 days out," Mr. Trump said last week.

The president has recently revived his "enemy of the people" line about the mainstream news media, sprinkling the phrase into his public remarks. The new White House communications chief, Bill Shine, a former president of Fox News, signaled a tougher approach to press relations when he barred a CNN reporter from a public event last week in the Rose Garden. The reason? She asked questions of Mr. Trump in what the White House deemed an inappropriate manner for an event in the Oval Office.

The approach may appall some journalism advocates, but it has buoyed many members of the president's base. Sean Hannity, perhaps Mr. Trump's most reliable defender on cable news, directly addressed Mr. Acosta on Tuesday night at the start of his program on Fox News.

"The people of this country, they're screaming at you for a reason," Mr. Hannity said. "They don't like your unfair, abusively biased treatment of the president of the United States."

A montage — titled "CNN's Jim Acosta Lowlights" — followed, with footage of Mr. Acosta pressing Ms. Sanders at briefings and criticizing the administration's attitude toward the news media.

"That's called opinion," Mr. Hannity said, when the camera came back to him. "And you're extremely rude. Oh, and a liberal partisan hack. That's why Americans don't trust you and fake news CNN."

Press freedom groups have long warned that Mr. Trump's rhetoric — and the accompanying criticism from his supporters — is endangering journalists domestically and abroad, particularly under autocratic regimes that have adopted his language in cracking down on independent journalism.

Those concerns came up during a meeting last month between Mr. Trump and the publisher of The New York Times, A. G. Sulzberger, who asked the president to reconsider his use of the term "enemy of the people."

After that meeting was made public last Sunday — Mr. Trump, ignoring the White House's off-the-record stipulation, tweeted about it — the president opened a new flank of attack. He wrote on Twitter that reporters who reveal "internal deliberations of our government" are putting "the lives of many, not just journalists, at risk!"

Ms. Sanders picked up on that theme at her briefing on Wednesday, the press secretary's first question-and-answer session with reporters in nine days. (Ms. Sanders held only three formal news briefings in July, compared with nearly once a day in the early part of her tenure.)

"The media routinely reports on classified information and government secrets that put lives in danger and risk valuable national security tools," Ms. Sanders told reporters, going on to cite a debunked story that a report about Osama bin Laden in the 1990s had harmed national intelligence efforts. (President George W. Bush has made the same claim, that a report about Bin Laden's use of a satellite phone had tipped him off to surveillance; the information had been released by the Taliban two years earlier.)

"It's now standard to abandon common sense ethical practices," Ms. Sanders continued. "This is a two-way street. We certainly support a free press, we certainly condemn violence against anybody, but we also ask that people act responsibly and report accurately and fairly."

‘You Are a Rude, Terrible Person’: After Midterms, Trump Renews His Attacks on the Press

BY MICHAEL M. GRYNBAUM | NOV. 7, 2018

PRESIDENT TRUMP lashed out at journalists during a surly and contentious news conference at the White House on Wednesday, renewing his attacks on the news media as “the enemy of the people” just moments after pledging an end to partisan politics in the wake of a grueling midterm election.

In tense exchanges on live television, Mr. Trump denounced a network correspondent as “very rude,” sternly told several reporters to “sit down,” and at one point stepped away from his lectern, suggesting that he was prepared to cut off the session — a rare formal East Room news conference — because of queries he disliked.

Not for the first time, Mr. Trump appeared most incensed by a question from Jim Acosta of CNN, who challenged Mr. Trump’s characterization of a caravan of migrants in Mexico as an imminent “invasion.”

“Honestly, I think you should let me run the country — you run CNN,” Mr. Trump replied, his voice rising. “And if you did it well, your ratings would be much better.”

When Mr. Acosta attempted a follow-up, about the special counsel’s investigation into Russia and the Trump campaign, the president’s patience — what little was left — evaporated.

“That’s enough, that’s enough,” Mr. Trump said. “Put down the mic.”

As cameras rolled, a White House aide leaned toward Mr. Acosta and attempted to remove the microphone from his hands. Mr. Acosta held on (“Pardon me, ma’am”) and declined to sit, as Mr. Trump continued to berate him.

“CNN should be ashamed of itself, having you working for them,” the president said. “You are a rude, terrible person. You shouldn’t be working for CNN." He added, in a reference to the White House press secretary: "The way you treat Sarah Huckabee is horrible. You shouldn't treat people that way."

Jabbing a finger in the reporter's direction, he said, "When you report fake news, which CNN does a lot, you are the enemy of the people."

The president frequently clashes with reporters, particularly Mr. Acosta, whose confrontational style has sometimes rankled his press-room colleagues. But Mr. Trump also enjoys the jousting of a live news conference, and he had submitted to a string of interviews in the run-up to Tuesday's vote.

By Wednesday, though, with his party on its heels after having lost control of the House, Mr. Trump seemed more ornery than outgoing.

"Sit down!" he shouted several times as April Ryan, a correspondent for American Urban Radio Networks, tried to ask a question about voter suppression. "I didn't call you. I didn't call you. I'll give you voter suppression. Take a look at the CNN polls and how inaccurate they were."

As Ms. Ryan persisted, Mr. Trump kept up his scolding. "Such a hostile media, it's so sad," he said, accusing Ms. Ryan of interrupting a male reporter's question. "You rudely interrupted him. You rudely interrupted him."

Later, when Yamiche Alcindor of PBS asked about Mr. Trump and white nationalists, the president called her question "racist." "What you said is so insulting to me," he told Ms. Alcindor, who, like Ms. Ryan, is a woman of color.

"I followed up the president calling my question 'racist' with a policy question about his proposed middle class tax cut because that's what journalists do," Ms. Alcindor wrote on Twitter after the exchange. "We press on. We focus on the privilege of asking questions for a living. We do the work."

Attacking the press usually redounds to Mr. Trump's benefit: Many of his supporters are fired up by denunciations of news organizations as liberal elites. Jon Favreau, the "Pod Save America" host and former aide to President Barack Obama, lamented Wednesday's exchanges as playing into the president's hands.

"Can we not make today into another Trump v. Media fight?" Mr. Favreau wrote on Twitter. "This is exactly what he wants."

The president's "enemy of the people" language has been blamed for the rising number of threats against journalists, and press freedom groups say Mr. Trump's words have emboldened autocrats around the world to crack down on reporters. CNN issued a statement on Wednesday standing by Mr. Acosta and calling Mr. Trump's attacks on the news media "disturbingly un-American."

"While President Trump has made it clear he does not respect a free press, he has a sworn obligation to protect it," the network said.

Mr. Trump has expressed little sympathy for those concerns. On Wednesday, he ended his appearance by saying, "It isn't good what the media is doing."

"I am being treated very unfairly," he said, "and I'm fighting back not for me, but for the people of this country."

At one point Peter Alexander of NBC News piped up in Mr. Acosta's defense, telling the president that he was "a hard-working, diligent reporter" who "busts his butt."

Mr. Trump shot Mr. Alexander a look. "I'm not a big fan of yours, either, to be honest," the president said.

Even in a tense room filled with journalists, the line earned some laughs.

CNN Sues Trump Administration for Barring Jim Acosta From White House

BY MICHAEL M. GRYNBAUM | NOV. 13, 2018

CNN SUED THE Trump administration on Tuesday in an effort to reinstate the press credentials of its chief White House correspondent, Jim Acosta, escalating a dispute that has highlighted the increasingly tense dynamic between President Trump and the news media.

In a lawsuit filed in Federal District Court, the network argued that the removal of Mr. Acosta's White House press pass constituted a violation of his First Amendment rights to freely report on the government. CNN also asserted that the administration had violated Mr. Acosta's due process rights guaranteed by the Fifth Amendment when it revoked his credentials without warning.

Mr. Acosta, who has frequently clashed with Mr. Trump, angered the president at a formal news conference last week with questions about immigration and the special counsel's investigation. The CNN correspondent would not give up the microphone after Mr. Trump tried to move on to another reporter.

Hours later, the press secretary, Sarah Huckabee Sanders, announced that the administration had removed Mr. Acosta's credentials, which allowed him access to the White House grounds. The administration falsely claimed that Mr. Acosta had placed his hands on a White House intern who had tried to take his microphone away during the news conference.

"While the suit is specific to CNN and Acosta, this could have happened to anyone," CNN said in a statement. "If left unchallenged, the actions of the White House would create a dangerous chilling effect for any journalist who covers our elected officials."

A hearing on the lawsuit was set for Wednesday at 3:30 p.m. The judge in the case is Timothy J. Kelly, who was nominated last year by President Trump and then approved by the Senate.

Shortly after the lawsuit was filed, the White House responded with a statement. “This is just more grandstanding from CNN, and we will vigorously defend against this lawsuit,” Ms. Sanders wrote, noting that dozens of other CNN journalists have retained their White House credentials.

Ms. Sanders made no mention of her original claim that Mr. Acosta had reacted inappropriately with the intern. Instead, she wrote that “he physically refused to surrender a White House microphone to an intern, so that other reporters might ask their questions.”

“The White House cannot run an orderly and fair press conference when a reporter acts this way, which is neither appropriate nor professional,” she added.

In turning to the courts, CNN has taken perhaps the most aggressive action yet by a news organization against a president.

Mr. Trump has vilified the press since he started running for office in 2015. His denigration of the news media as “the enemy of the American people” — and his popularization of “fake news” as a way to dismiss critical coverage — has alarmed press freedom groups around the world.

Supporters of Mr. Trump, though, are likely to seize on the lawsuit as evidence for the president’s claim that news organizations, especially CNN, are biased against him. “CNN sucks!” has been a frequent chant at Mr. Trump’s rallies. The reporter Bob Woodward, speaking in Florida on Tuesday, said that a lawsuit may play into Mr. Trump’s hands.

“I think Trump would sit around and look at this and say, ‘This is great,’ ” Mr. Woodward said onstage at the Global Financial Leadership Conference. “Nixon effectively made the conduct of the media the issue, rather than his conduct. Trump has adopted that strategy, he’s refined it. It’s very effective, and so when we engage in it, we’re taking his bait, in my view.”

Floyd Abrams, the noted First Amendment lawyer, said in an interview on Tuesday that CNN’s legal action was necessary, even as he acknowledged the potential political fallout.

"I can understand the reluctance — at a time when the president is saying, 'CNN is hostile to me' — for a lawsuit to be filed with the caption 'CNN v. Donald Trump,' " Mr. Abrams said. "That said, sometimes a strong response is necessary, both for the institution itself and for the broader cause for which it effectively speaks."

Mr. Acosta, who has a reputation as a showboat among some of his press corps colleagues, is not the first White House reporter to aggressively question a president in public. One of his predecessors, the ABC correspondent Sam Donaldson, said in a memo filed with CNN's lawsuit that he knew of no precedent for a journalist's credentials being withdrawn and "never would have imagined such action was possible."

Still, rival networks have not issued formal statements in support of CNN or Mr. Acosta. The White House Correspondents' Association on Tuesday criticized the removal of Mr. Acosta's credential, but did not address the lawsuit itself.

"Revoking access to the White House complex amounted to disproportionate reaction to the events of last Wednesday," the group's president, Olivier Knox of SiriusXM radio, wrote. "The president of the United States should not be in the business of arbitrarily picking the men and women who cover him."

CNN's argument for restoring Mr. Acosta's credential resembles a lawsuit in 1977 that involved Robert Sherrill, then a correspondent for The Nation magazine who was denied a White House press pass. A court ruled that the Secret Service had to follow a clear process, including prior written notice, before revoking a journalist's credentials, a precedent cited on Tuesday by CNN's legal team.

Andrew Napolitano, a former Superior Court judge in New Jersey and sometime Trump confidant, said on Tuesday that he expected CNN to prevail. "Obviously, Acosta may have been an irritant to the president, but he was hardly a danger to him," Mr. Napolitano said on the Fox Business Network. "CNN's got a very good case. I think this will be resolved quickly. I don't expect a jury trial."

Ms. Sanders is named as a defendant in the suit, along with Mr. Trump; his chief of staff, John Kelly; the head of White House communications strategy, Bill Shine; and the Secret Service.

The lawsuit states that Jeff Zucker, CNN's president, personally wrote to Mr. Kelly last Thursday asking for Mr. Acosta's press pass to be reinstated. Mr. Zucker also accused the administration of a "pattern of targeted harassment" against journalists from CNN.

CNN also said in the suit that Mr. Acosta was prevented from covering parts of Mr. Trump's weekend trip to Paris, and that his request last Thursday for a temporary day pass to the White House was rejected.

CNN's corporate parent, AT&T, remains embroiled in its own legal battle with the administration.

The Justice Department filed a federal appeal in July to unravel AT&T's merger with Time Warner, which owns CNN. Arguments in that case are scheduled to be heard on Dec. 6. The government had tried to block the deal before it was approved by a federal judge in June.

The law firm Gibson, Dunn & Crutcher is representing CNN in the Acosta lawsuit. The legal team includes Theodore B. Olson, who served as solicitor general under former President George W. Bush. Mr. Trump previously tried to hire Mr. Olson for his own legal team, without success.

MAGGIE HABERMAN contributed reporting.

CNN's Jim Acosta Has Press Pass Restored by White House

BY MICHAEL M. GRYNBAUM | NOV. 19, 2018

JIM ACOSTA HAS his press pass back.

The Trump administration stood down on Monday from its nearly two-week-long dispute with CNN over the White House credentials of Mr. Acosta, informing the correspondent that his badge was formally restored. CNN in turn dropped its lawsuit on the matter, which had ballooned into a test of press freedoms in the Trump era.

But while it yielded to Mr. Acosta — whose testy questions had touched off Mr. Trump's ire — the administration used the occasion to lay down a set of formal rules governing reporters' behavior at future White House news conferences, a highly unusual step.

Among the guidelines was a restriction of one question per reporter, with follow-ups allowed at the discretion of the president or the White House official at the lectern. "Failure to abide," the administration warned, "may result in suspension or revocation of the journalist's hard pass."

The White House sought to blame Mr. Acosta for behaving disrespectfully, although Mr. Trump often lobs insults at journalists and encourages a free-for-all format when taking questions from reporters.

Codifying the behavior of journalists struck some as an ominous encroachment into freedom of the press, and the White House Correspondents' Association said on Monday that it had not been consulted about the new guidelines.

The American Civil Liberties Union, in a statement, said: "These rules give the White House far too much discretion to avoid real scrutiny. The White House belongs to the public, not the president, and the job of the press is to ask hard questions, not to be polite company."

Still, the guidelines are not far removed from the manner in which White House news conferences typically proceed. Mr. Trump made

SARAH SILBIGER/THE NEW YORK TIMES

A dispute over a White House press pass for the CNN correspondent Jim Acosta developed into a test of press freedoms in the Trump era.

clear last week that he would introduce "regulations" after a federal judge criticized the White House for stripping Mr. Acosta's credentials without due process or a coherent rationale.

"We would have greatly preferred to continue hosting White House press conferences in reliance on a set of understood professional norms, and we believe the overwhelming majority of journalists covering the White House share that preference," Sarah Huckabee Sanders, the press secretary, said in a statement.

Press relations were not always rosy in pre-Trump days. President Barack Obama's aides preselected the news outlets that were allowed to ask questions at his news conferences. Mr. Obama often chastised reporters, including Mr. Acosta on one occasion, for questions he deemed overly aggressive or grandstanding.

But Mr. Trump, a devoted news consumer who relishes his coverage, plays up his conflicts with reporters in part to excite his supporters. He has held far fewer formal news conferences than his predecessors, and the daily White House briefing has virtually disappeared on his watch.

Revoking Mr. Acosta's White House badge was the most severe step yet, and it soon became apparent that the move would not pass legal muster: After suing last week, Mr. Acosta was granted the temporary return of his credentials by a federal judge.

A back-and-forth ensued over the weekend. Bill Shine, the deputy chief of staff for communications, sent a letter to Mr. Acosta that listed several reasons that his pass had been revoked, perhaps an attempt to satisfy the judge's request for a clear rationale. CNN's lawyers called the note an "after-the-fact concocted process." By Monday afternoon, the sides had reached a resolution.

Aides to Mr. Trump say that the president does not mind answering questions, pointing to his numerous impromptu sessions with reporters during White House photo-ops and Marine One departures. The aides complain about reporters who they say do not respect the solemnity of the setting, even as Mr. Trump flouts many of the norms associated with his office.

"The White House's interaction is, and generally should be, subject to a natural give-and-take," Ms. Sanders wrote on Monday, suggesting that the onus was on the press corps to ensure that a "code of conduct" did not become necessary.

That notion read more like a warning — behave or else — and the Correspondents' Association seemed unmoved.

"For as long as there have been White House press conferences, White House reporters have asked follow-up questions," the group wrote on Monday. "We fully expect this tradition will continue."

Glossary

censorship Suppression or prohibition of news or information that is perceived as threatening, obscene or unacceptable.

digital media The distribution of digitized content via the Internet.

fake news A fictional story presented in the style of a legitimate news story, intended to deceive readers; also a phrase commonly used to discredit legitimate news because of its perspective on a subject.

First Amendment An amendment to the U.S. Constitution that prohibits limitations of freedoms with respect to speech, religion, expression, assembly or the right to petition the government.

freedom of the press Protected under the First Amendment; the right to circulate opinions without censorship.

impartiality A principle of journalism that a story should be balanced and not reflect the bias of the journalist.

legislation A law or set of laws.

media The main means of mass communication (radio and television broadcasting, newspaper and magazine publishing, and the Internet), regarded collectively.

press Newspapers and journalists, collectively.

press pass A pass that grants access to journalists.

reliability The dependability and accuracy of a journalistic source.

source The origin of the information reported in journalism.

surveillance Close watch kept over something or someone, typically without their knowledge.

Media Literacy Terms

"Media literacy" refers to the ability to access, understand, critically assess and create media. The following terms are important components of media literacy, and they will help you critically engage with the articles in this title

angle The aspect of a news story that a journalist focuses on and develops.

balance Principle of journalism that both perspectives of an argument should be presented in a fair way.

bias A disposition of prejudice in favor of a certain idea, person or perspective.

byline Name of the writer, usually placed between the headline and the story.

commentary Type of story that is an expression of opinion on recent events by a journalist generally known as a commentator.

credibility The quality of being trustworthy and believable, said of a journalistic source.

intention The motive or reason behind something, such as the publication of a news story.

motive The reason behind something, such as the publication of a news story or a source's perspective on an issue.

plagiarism An attempt to pass another person's work as one's own without attribution.

tone A manner of expression in writing or speech.

Media Literacy Questions

1. In "The Covert War" (on page 26), The New York Times paraphrases information from and directly quotes The Pentagon Papers. What are the strengths of the use of a paraphrase as opposed to a direct quote? What are the weaknesses?

2. "The Pentagon Papers Team Tells How The Times Defied Censorship" (on page 53) is an example of an interview. Can you identify skills or techniques used by interviewer David Dunlap and compiler Nancy Wartik to gather information from Allan Siegal, Linda Amster, Betsy Wade and James Goodale?

3. What type of story is "The Times and Wen Ho Lee" (on page 63)? Can you identify another article in this collection that is the same type of story? What elements helped you come to your conclusion?

4. Does John Collins Rudolf demonstrate the journalistic principle of balance in his article "Climate Questions and Fox News" (on page 81)? If so, how did he do so? If not, what could he have included to make the article more balanced?

5. The article "Why the Latest Layoffs are Devastating to Democracy" (on page 127) is an example of an op-ed. Identify how Farhad Manjoo's attitude and tone help convey his opinion on the topic.

6. What is the intention of the article "One Thing Donald Trump Would Like Is Freedom From the Press" (on page 195)? How effectively does it achieve its intended purpose?

Citations

All citations in this list are formatted according to the Modern Language Association's (MLA) style guide.

BOOK CITATION

THE NEW YORK TIMES EDITORIAL STAFF. *Journalism: The Need for a Free Press.* New York: New York Times Educational Publishing, 2020.

ONLINE ARTICLE CITATIONS

BAZELON, EMILY. "Billionaires vs. the Press in the Era of Trump." *The New York Times*, 22 Nov. 2016, https://www.nytimes.com/2016/11/22/magazine/billionaires-vs-the-press-in-the-era-of-trump.html.

CARR, DAVID. "David Carr's Last Word on Journalism, Aimed at Students." *The New York Times*, 15 Feb. 2015, https://www.nytimes.com/2015/02/16/business/media/david-carr-as-a-passionate-professor-shaping-the-future-of-journalism.html.

CHOZICK, AMY. "After Mueller Report, News Media Leaders Defend Their Work." *The New York Times*, 25 Mar. 2019, https://www.nytimes.com/2019/03/25/business/media/mueller-report-media.html.

DUNLAP, DAVID W. "1971 | Supreme Court Allows Publication of Pentagon Papers." *The New York Times*, 30 June 2016, https://www.nytimes.com/2016/06/30/insider/1971-supreme-court-allows-publication-of-pentagon-papers.html.

EDSALL, THOMAS B. "One Thing Donald Trump Would Like Is Freedom From the Press." *The New York Times*, 15 Mar. 2018, https://www.nytimes.com/2018/03/15/opinion/trump-press-freedom-fake-news.html.

ERVIN, SAM J., JR. "The Freedom to Speak." *The New York Times*, 3 Oct. 1971, https://www.nytimes.com/1971/10/03/archives/the-freedom-to-speak.html.

FORTIN, JACEY. "In Final Column, Jamal Khashoggi Laments Dearth of Free Press in Arab World." *The New York Times*, 17 Oct. 2018, https://www.nytimes.com/2018/10/17/business/media/jamal-khashoggi-washington-post.html.

FRANKEL, MAX. "150th Anniversary: 1851-2001; Turning Away From the Holocaust." *The New York Times*, 14 Nov. 2001, https://www.nytimes.com/2001/11/14/news/150th-anniversary-1851-2001-turning-away-from-the-holocaust.html.

FRENCH, HOWARD W. "The Legacy of Simeon Booker, a Pioneer of Civil Rights Journalism." *The New York Times*, 13 Dec. 2017, https://www.nytimes.com/2017/12/13/opinion/simeon-booker-civil-rights-journalism.html.

FRIENDLY, FRED W. "A 45-Year-Old Rivet in the First Amendment." *The New York Times*, 9 June 1976, https://www.nytimes.com/1976/06/09/archives/a-45yearold-rivet-in-the-first-amendment.html.

GLADSTONE, RICK, AND SHREEYA SINHA. "Steven Sotloff, Journalist Held by ISIS, Was Undeterred by Risks of Job." *The New York Times*, 22 Aug. 2014, https://www.nytimes.com/2014/08/23/world/middleeast/steven-sotloff.html.

GRYNBAUM, MICHAEL M. "CNN's Jim Acosta Has Press Pass Restored by White House." *The New York Times*, 19 Nov. 2018, https://www.nytimes.com/2018/11/19/business/media/jim-acosta-press-pass-cnn.html.

GRYNBAUM, MICHAEL M. "CNN Sues Trump Administration for Barring Jim Acosta From White House." *The New York Times*, 13 Nov. 2018, https://www.nytimes.com/2018/11/13/business/media/cnn-jim-acosta-trump-lawsuit.html.

GRYNBAUM, MICHAEL M. "Crowds, Stoked by Trump's Rhetoric, Increase Their Ire Toward the Press." *The New York Times*, 1 Aug. 2018, https://www.nytimes.com/2018/08/01/business/media/trump-press-jim-acosta.html.

GRYNBAUM, MICHAEL M. " 'You Are a Rude, Terrible Person': After Midterms, Trump Renews His Attacks on the Press." *The New York Times*, 7 Nov. 2018, https://www.nytimes.com/2018/11/07/business/media/trump-press-conference-media.html.

HAAG, MATTHEW. "Former Fox News Analyst Calls Network a 'Destructive Propaganda Machine.' " *The New York Times*, 7 June 2018, https://www.nytimes.com/2018/06/07/business/media/ralph-peters-fox-cnn.html.

HABERMAN, CLYDE. "Amid Leaks, Recalling an Epic Battle Over Press Freedom in Nixon Era." *The New York Times*, 26 Mar. 2017, https://www.nytimes.com/2017/03/26/us/trump-secrets-nixon-pentagon-papers.html.

HAUGHNEY, CHRISTINE. "Bezos, Amazon's Founder, to Buy The Washington Post." *The New York Times*, 5 Aug. 2013, https://www.nytimes.com/2013/08/06/business/media/amazoncom-founder-to-buy-the-washington-post.html.

JOHNSTON, NEAL. "Colonel McCormick to the Rescue." *The New York Times*, 12 July 1981, https://www.nytimes.com/1981/07/12/books/colonel-mccormick-to-the-rescue.html.

KRISTOF, NICHOLAS. "When Reporting Is Dangerous." *The New York Times*, 3 Sept. 2014, https://www.nytimes.com/2014/09/04/opinion/when-reporting-is-dangerous.html.

LEE, EDMUND. "Digital Media: What Went Wrong." *The New York Times*, 1 Feb. 2019, https://www.nytimes.com/2019/02/01/business/media/buzzfeed-digital-media-wrong.html.

LEONHARDT, DAVID. "The Six Forms of Media Bias." *The New York Times*, 31 Jan. 2019, https://www.nytimes.com/2019/01/31/opinion/media-bias-howard-schultz.html.

LEWIS, ANTHONY. "At Home Abroad; Freedom of the Press." *The New York Times*, 7 June 1981, https://www.nytimes.com/1981/06/07/opinion/at-home-abroad-freedom-of-the-press.html.

MANJOO, FARHAD. "Why the Latest Layoffs Are Devastating to Democracy." *The New York Times*, 30 Jan. 2019, https://www.nytimes.com/2019/01/30/opinion/buzzfeed-layoffs.html.

THE NEW-YORK SUN. "A Candid Opinion." *The New York Times*, 1 Nov. 1875, https://www.nytimes.com/1875/11/01/archives/a-candid-opinion-libel-suits-and-the-newyork-times-the-freedom-of.html.

THE NEW YORK TIMES. "The Covert War." *The New York Times*, 13 June 1971, https://www.nytimes.com/1971/06/13/archives/the-covert-war.html.

THE NEW YORK TIMES. "Death by Terror." *The New York Times*, 21 Aug. 2014, https://www.nytimes.com/2014/08/22/opinion/james-foleys-execution-and-the-question-of-ransom.html.

THE NEW YORK TIMES. "Free But Responsible." *The New York Times*, 3 June 1931, https://www.nytimes.com/1931/06/03/archives/free-but-responsible.html.

THE NEW YORK TIMES. "Freedom of the Press." *The New York Times*, 8 Sept. 1861, https://www.nytimes.com/1861/09/08/archives/freedom-of-the-press.html.

THE NEW YORK TIMES. "The Freedom of the Press." *The New York Times*, 19 Oct. 1873, https://www.nytimes.com/1873/10/19/archives/the-freedom-of-the-press.html.

THE NEW YORK TIMES. "The Freedom of the Press." *The New York Times*, 30 May 1917, https://www.nytimes.com/1917/05/30/archives/the-freedom-of-the-press.html.

THE NEW YORK TIMES. "From the Editors; The Times and Iraq." *The New York Times*, 26 May 2004, https://www.nytimes.com/2004/05/26/world/from-the-editors-the-times-and-iraq.html.

THE NEW YORK TIMES. "Journalism." *The New York Times*, 11 Oct. 1851, https://www.nytimes.com/1851/10/11/archives/journalism.html.

THE NEW YORK TIMES. "The Times and Wen Ho Lee." *The New York Times*, 26 Sept. 2000, https://www.nytimes.com/2000/09/26/nyregion/the-times-and-wen-ho-lee.html.

RICE, ANDREW. "Putting a Price on Words." *The New York Times*, 12 May 2010, https://www.nytimes.com/2010/05/16/magazine/16Journalism-t.html.

RUDOLF, JOHN COLLINS. "Climate Questions and Fox News." *The New York Times*, 17 Dec. 2010, https://green.blogs.nytimes.com/2010/12/17/climate-questions-and-fox-news/.

RUTENBERG, JIM. "Independent Press Is Under Siege as Freedom Rings." *The New York Times*, 2 July 2017, https://www.nytimes.com/2017/07/02/business/media/independent-press-is-under-siege-as-freedom-rings.html.

RUTENBERG, JIM. "Trump Takes Aim at the Press, With a Flamethrower." *The New York Times*, 23 Aug. 2017, https://www.nytimes.com/2017/08/23/business/media/trump-takes-aim-at-the-press-with-a-flamethrower.html.

RUTENBERG, JIM. "Where Will Trump Stand on Press Freedoms?" *The New York Times*, 13 Nov. 2016, https://www.nytimes.com/2016/11/14/business/media/where-will-trump-stand-on-press-freedoms.html.

SIMON, JOEL. "Trump Is Damaging Press Freedom in the U.S. and Abroad." *The New York Times*, 25 Feb. 2017, https://www.nytimes.com/2017/02/25/opinion/trump-is-damaging-press-freedom-in-the-us-and-abroad.html.

SOMAIYA, RAVI. "How Facebook Is Changing the Way Its Users Consume Journalism." *The New York Times*, 26 Oct. 2014, https://www.nytimes.com/2014/10/27/business/media/how-facebook-is-changing-the-way-its-users-consume-journalism.html.

SPAYD, LIZ. "Why Readers See The Times as Liberal." *The New York Times*, 23 July 2016, https://www.nytimes.com/2016/07/24/public-editor/liz-spayd-the-new-york-times-public-editor.html.

SULLIVAN, MARGARET. "Lessons in a Surveillance Drama Redux." *The New York Times*, 9 Nov. 2013, https://www.nytimes.com/2013/11/10/public-editor/sullivan-lessons-in-a-surveillance-drama-redux.html.

SYMONDS, ALEXANDRIA, AND KATIE VAN SYCKLE. "How Two Times Reporters Pieced Together Allegations Against Ryan Adams." *The New York Times*, 21 Feb. 2019, https://www.nytimes.com/2019/02/21/reader-center/ryan-adams-investigation.html.

WADLER, JOYCE. "Fighting for Press Freedom in a Dangerous World." *The New York Times*, 27 Feb. 2002, https://www.nytimes.com/2002/02/27/nyregion/public-lives-fighting-for-press-freedom-in-a-dangerous-world.html.

WARTIK, NANCY. "The Pentagon Papers Team Tells How The Times Defied Censorship." *The New York Times*, 20 Jan. 2018, https://www.nytimes.com/2018/01/20/reader-center/history-of-pentagon-papers.html.

Index

This book is current up until the time of printing. For the most up-to-date reporting, visit www.nytimes.com.